LIVE YOUR
LIFE FROM THE
INSIDE
OUT

LIVE YOUR
LIFE FROM THE
INSIDE
OUT

Unlocking the Power of
*the **DIVINE COACH** Within*

Maureen McIntosh-Alberts, PhD

Walton Publishing House
Houston, Texas
www.waltonpublishinghouse.com
Printed in the United States of America

Disclaimer: The advice found within may not be suitable for every individual. This work is purchased with the understanding that neither the author nor the publisher is held responsible for any results. Neither author nor publisher assumes responsibility for errors, omissions, or contrary interpretations of the subject matter herein. Any perceived disparagement of an individual or organization is a misinterpretation.

Brand and product names mentioned are trademarks that belong solely to their respective owners. Library of Congress Cataloging-in-Publication Data under

ISBN: 978-1-953993-35-9 (Paperback)
ISBN: 978-1-953993-34-2 (Digital)

CONTENTS

FOREWORD

The old adage that "Life is what YOU make it" is true in every context of the word. Our capacity as human beings to exercise free will is illustrative that we have the wherewithal within each of us to make or construct our lives to our liking, or even to the wishes of certain others, and to then duly live out our choices. WE are indisputably in the driver's seat, steering our life's courses of action. Notwithstanding, there is a glaring question that we should all ask ourselves daily - how proficient of a driver am I on the avenue of life?

As King for the Se (Shai) State in Ghana, a University Chancellor, the Visionary Founder of Life International, and an advisor/mentor to countless many around the globe; my primary regard, even before matters of self, is for the lives and welfare of those for whom I am responsible, and who count on me for guidance. People look to me as an authority on life issues, and I must always be readily able to assess, enlighten, and direct individuals through life decisions and challenges. Over many years and across a spectrum of persons and situations encountered, I have observed consistently that people are most proficient in the "driver's seat" of life when they've fully accepted that they, and NO one else, are in control of and answerable for the state of their existence. Ownership of one's choices and actions is the first step in the pursuit of a well-lived life.

The book, *Live Your Life from the Inside Out*, is a brilliant resource on revolutionizing your life by first knowing your significance and learning how to rely on the insight resident within you. The concept of taking ownership of our lives, and progressing on to purposefully look within ourselves, is extremely practical as life is essentially a compilation of our most dominant thoughts, and the dreams to which we aspire.

I have known the author, Dr. Maureen McIntosh-Alberts for over 15 years, and have had the opportunity to witness her distinctive gift of life coaching and molding leaders, which she carries out in utmost excellence. The principles she shares in *Live Your Life from the Inside Out* are ingenious, yet timeless, on point, functional, nurturing in nature, and transcends all age groups, genders, genres, and life experiences. Dr. McIntosh-Alberts has an astuteness as only a select few do in the profession of Leadership Training to help others come face to face with themselves and to trust their instincts in life matters. This captivating book will inspire and empower individuals to excavate unexplored abilities, talents, and confidence from the layers of their being as a skilled archeologist does artifacts from a historical site.

Live Your Life from the Inside Out is an absolute must-read. It's profound in content while easy to comprehend and follow in application. I highly recommend its transforming principles. Go ahead and dare to escape from a mediocre existence to an intentional, purposeful, and rewarding life – the choice is yours. Dr. McIntosh-Alberts, is the Life Coach waiting to avidly show you how to be in the driver's seat of your life!

HRM King Drolor Bosso Adamtey I Suapolor - Se Matse
Ghana

FOREWORD

As I read the captivating pages of this book, I am compelled to pay homage to God, Jesus, and the Holy Spirit all of whom have influenced the work of Dr. Maureen McIntosh-Alberts, a mighty woman of God who definitely listens to the Holy Spirit and *lives her life from the inside out*. In addition to that, she coaches others to "Unlock the Power of the Divine Coach Within" and has become one of the most prolific spiritual minds of our time. *How do I know?* Glad you asked. I have had the privilege of being "coached" by this dynamic, empowering, and intentional person who has helped thousands to become the "best version of themselves," including me. I, too, have become more spirit-led, intentional, and have deepened my relationship with the Holy Spirit; learned to abandon parts of my belief system to become more conscious of choices I was making that were holding me back from living the best version of myself. For one year, I opened myself up to new ways of thinking; new ways of responding rather than reacting. In short, I learned to do a closer self-analysis of where I was; where I wanted to be and asking myself, what can I do to change the results I am having? Through our individual, group, and quarterly summit sessions, I learned the tools, principles, and strategies needed to shift my life into alignment with the "Divine Coach." And, throughout this book, you can learn to do so as well.

I learned to incorporate "The Principles of Intentional Living" into my life throughout our year long coaching sessions. As I pondered on the words *life doesn't give you what you want; life gives you who you are*—no words, other than God's Word, were ever more truthful. When we think about Dr. Maureen's challenge "to go within and respond to three questions she outlines for accessing your potential; it will cause you to take some time to examine whether or not you are committed to intentional living. When I examined myself and those three questions, I knew beyond a doubt that I had to stretch beyond my own "comfort zone" be more willing to share my life story; to do something that makes a difference, and be urgent about utilizing my own God-given talents; to connect with more like-minded people and partner with life-valued people—after reading this book, I believe you, too will see the value of "why good intentions aren't enough" and you, too, will learn to search until you find your "why" which I believe Dr. Maureen is alluding to when she asks those three critical questions in Chapter II and outlines the Principles of Intentional Living.

Further, the section on *Living a Life of Significance* invites us to examine if we are indeed living a life of significance—not fame or fortune but making a difference right where you are. I learned this requires us to tap into our "why." Throughout the book, threads of "why" can be seen, which is simply asking what your life's purpose is. To borrow a quote from John Maxwell, he says "purpose is like a snowball—it builds over time." Dr. Maureen helps you to find your purpose and to become more intentional about fulfilling God's purpose for your life, not what you want; but asking the Holy Spirit to guide you. She challenges you to listen to the Holy Spirit; to invite the Holy Spirit into your life, and to live your life for our Lord and Savior. In doing so, the Holy Spirit of God will open every door so that you can expand your resilience capacity; experience abundance in every dimension of your life: spiritual, personal, physical, emotional, relational, financial, and professional. Over the course of the past year, each of these dimensions of my life has significantly improved; no doubt, this book will assist you in doing the same.

Utilizing her God-given gifts through this authorship, Dr. Maureen gives wisdom, insight, and direction in helping us to fully understand the role of the Holy Spirit in our lives and its importance to our becoming the best version of ourselves. You will find piercing, thought-provoking questions that ask you to "dig deeper" and yes, I found that I, too, had to "fasten my spiritual and mental seatbelt" as Dr. Maureen engages us and enlightens us on the Holy Spirit and the fact that He is our "Divine Coach." WOW! A very compelling, fascinating, powerful, convincing, and persuasive book, which will lead you to an experience that will require you to stop any limiting beliefs; to make the necessary sacrifices to bring forth your God-given talents and purpose; and to expand your potential to, in the words of Dr. Maureen, "live a life of fulfillment and significance. So, dig deep and hold on; I guarantee, you are in for a life-changing experience; one that you will not soon forget!"

Brenda "BJ" Jarmon, PhD
Educator, Author and Consultant

FOREWORD

Live Your Life from the Inside Out: Unlocking the Power of the Divine Coach Within, written by Dr. Maureen McIntosh-Alberts, has the power to transform lives. Her step-by-step process guides the reader to go deeper within to better understand how life doesn't give you what you want but who you are. She helps the reader to explore from within how this happens and how you can create the life you want.

We each have our own and unique lived experiences. How often have we paused to take inventory of our life to see how we have created the life we have by our belief system that lies deep within? How much time, if ever, have we paused from the many cares and pursuits in life to understand what we believe and how our beliefs guide our behaviors and actions? Have we identified our self-limiting thoughts that lead to doubts and fears? Where could we be today if we could not only point to them, but we could eradicate them?

This is a book filled with wisdom and insights about how life has shaped us in ways that have limited us from living out or up to the full potential of how God created us. It is eye-opening to discover how we can limit ourselves and derail our own potential.

The overall focus of "Living Life from the Inside Out: Unlocking the Power of the Divine Coach Within," is transformative. Dr. Maureen, as I affectionately call her, guides the reader into a greater awareness of how external factors, societal influences, upbringing, traditions, education, and life itself have shaped us into being who we are today. She challenges us to explore more deeply to see how much more we are truly capable of and what we can do to live up to our fullest potential.

Dr. Maureen is capable of unlocking the power of the divine coach based on her knowledge and professional expertise in coaching. I have personally known Dr. Maureen for over twenty years, having had the honor of attending her commencement ceremony when she received a Ph.D. in Behavioral Science. She has effectively used her professional credentials at the World Bank and in other professional settings. However, I see her passion come alive when using her gift in transformational coaching, thereby helping others grow to become the best version of themselves. She is today a most notable professional coach. I have the honor of calling her my professional coach and was a participant in her inaugural mastermind inner circle coaching academy. Her life is guided by her faith and relationship with God which is evident by the ever-present fruit of the spirit.

Dr. Maureen is truly gifted in using her God-given passion, education, and experience in the behavioral sciences to provide transformative coaching to others. She writes with candor, forthrightness, and transparency in sharing her own lived experiences to guide the reader into a deeper understanding of self from the inside out. It is a writing and guidebook so desperately needed. The starting place to creating better homes, workplaces, and communities, begins by looking within ourselves. Dr. Maureen provides the roadmap to help us each become the best version of ourselves.

Dr. Adriene Wright

FOREWORD

D r. Maureen McIntosh-Alberts is eminently qualified to write on her chosen subject, the person and operations of the Holy Spirit. She has chosen to refer to Him in the nom-de-guerre, the Divine Coach, alluding to one of many roles He plays in the lives of those He touches.

Having studied and earned various degrees, including a PhD. from prestigious institutions, such as Johns Hopkins University, Georgetown University, Fuller Theological Seminary, to mention a few, Dr. Maureen is well trained and highly competent, as a thinker and as a teacher. These accolades, however, are not what qualify her to write on the Holy Spirit.

She has practiced for decades as a behavioral scientist, working with distinguished organizations such as The World Bank and the Organization of American States. Yet again, these experiences are not her basis for writing this book.

As a Seminary trained teacher of the Holy Writ, she is credentialed as a Reverend, and has been preaching for decades but still she does not see all that as sufficient criteria for embarking on this work.

Her motivation, which is also her qualification, can only be attributed to her long walk with the Holy Spirit. Dr. Maureen has enjoyed a thriving relationship with her Divine Coach for more than 5 decades. Having lived and studied bilingually, (English and Spanish) in several countries, this widowed mother and grandmother has had many ups and downs in her rich and storied life. What she learnt about the Holy Spirit in Bible School has been borne out by her many, many real-life experiences.

During the vicissitudes of her life, she has been taught, nourished, instructed, comforted, corrected and empowered and emboldened by the Holy Spirit. Her Divine Coach has guided her to many great accomplishments, a few of which are mentioned above. She has learned to depend on Him when life dealt her painful blows, including the loss of loved ones, the loss of social status and having to start life over as an immigrant in the US, with its attendant hardships.

She has kept her relationship with Him when she cried tears of sorrow and when she shed tears of joy.

Over the course of more than thirty years in the ministry of the gospel of our Lord Jesus Christ, I have had the privilege of meeting and ministering alongside many illustrious leaders, preachers and authors. No author compares to the Holy Spirit, the one who moved through the prophets who wrote the Holy Scriptures. Within that same time, I have learnt to recognize His unique voice, whenever he inspires contemporary speakers and writers. One such inspired person is the writer of this book.

I have had the blessed opportunity of knowing Dr. Maureen for about nine years, as a personal friend and as a colleague in the ministry. I can say unreservedly, that Dr. Maureen McIntosh-Alberts undoubtedly has an intimate knowledge of the Holy Spirit. Her vital knowledge has been gained through the multidimensional lens of long and serious study, both scriptural and secular, over many decades of actual life experiences.

She is worth listening to when she speaks or writes about the Divine Coach, God's Holy Spirit, the guide to a life, lived more abundantly.

This is a time in history, when change is happening so fast, even the experts can hardly keep up, much less understand things. Leaders and common people are all winging it, and floundering through life. Unabated acrimony, due to political and racial differences, seems to be the order of the day. Even Christians are caught in unending tendentious strife. There is no better time than now, for one to get seriously acquainted with the third person of the Godhead. I recommend this book as yet another means by which our gracious God chooses to enlarge our minds, enrich our lives and prepare us for the full manifestation of His glorious inheritance, through His Holy Spirit the earnest of our inheritance.

If you have never walked with the Holy Spirit, read this book and get introduced to Him by one who knows Him well.

If you have an ongoing relationship with the Holy Spirit, read this book and be enriched in your knowledge...

"There are different kinds of spiritual gifts, but the same Spirit is the source of them all. There are different kinds of service, but we serve the same Lord. God works in different ways, but it is the same God who does the work in all of us."

1 Corinthians 12:4-6
Rev. Niyi Adams
Sound Of the Word Ministries

PREFACE

The most misunderstood and perhaps the most abused person in the Godhead is the Holy Spirit. I know this is a shocking statement to begin this book with, but I stand by my statement. I believe that many people of the Christian faith do not know Him or what His function is in the Godhead and their lives. If you have picked up this book, I believe perhaps you feel the same way too. Or, maybe you don't know Him, and you desire to come to know the Holy Spirit and develop a personal relationship with Him.

Congratulations on your decision to do so. I promise you that by the time you have finished reading this book, you will come to know the Holy Spirit by putting the principles I share with you in this book into practice. You will also have developed a personal relationship with Him and go on to experience the abundant life, the fulfilled life of significance, and the life of freedom you desire for yourself and your loved ones. That life which Jesus Christ came to ensure you have.

If there was ever an urgency in the Body of Christ to fully understand the role of the Holy Spirit, it is now. In addition to the many diverse roles He plays in the life of believers, it's also important, even critical, I would say, for believers to come to know Him and to discover how they can partner with Him to live the abundant life Christ guarantees every believer. If you don't know Him, if you are not aware of the Holy Spirit's important role in your life, you will never experience success, prosperity, abundance, and significance.

I believe that because of this lack of knowledge, many believers are living a life way below their potential. Because of this lack of knowledge or, in some cases, unbelief, they will never be able to receive the Holy Spirit's power. They're struggling in every area – financially, emotionally, relationally, and spiritually. *It doesn't have to be this way.* Besides, this is a dangerous way to live. It's like playing Russian Roulette with your life, hoping and wishing things will magically align, but they never will. Why? Because that's just not how God created us to live.

Sadly, the Holy Spirit is a missing discussion for many in the body of Christ today. He was missing when I was growing up, and He is still missing and misunderstood today. As a young Catholic Christian girl, I did not know about Jesus Christ, nor did I have a relationship with Him or with the person of the Holy Spirit. As a result of my Catholic upbringing, my relationship was limited only to God the Father. Then, one day, I was introduced to Jesus Christ, and I gave my heart to Him. I had what is described as a born-again transformational spiritual experience, a new life, one that took my life in a totally new direction. From that day, which was a defining moment in my life, I wanted to know more about who Jesus was. So, I started studying the Bible to learn more about Jesus. At the start of my relationship with Jesus, I did not know who to pray to. I was confused. *Do I pray to the Father? Do I pray to Jesus? Which one of them was listening to me?* Since my original relationship was developed with God the Father, I had been used to praying to the Father. Now, I was told to pray to Jesus because He was my intercessor. It felt as though, in order to incorporate Jesus, I was abandoning my relationship with my Father and turning to Jesus. I did not realize that in order for the Father to hear and answer me, I needed to pray in the name of Jesus. I did not realize that the Biblical way to make my request known to God the Father was to call on God the Father as I did before but to do so using the name of Jesus. It took a while and much study of the Word of God, the Bible, to understand the concept of praying to the Father in the name of Jesus. However, as I continued to study the word, I finally got it. I am now comfortably praying to the Father in the name of Jesus.

In continuing my study of the Word of God, it came to my attention that there was also an important third person in the Godhead, the Holy Spirit. I was even more confused. *There are now three personalities?* I questioned. *How do they work?* This was just so mind-boggling; I could not understand how this worked with God, Jesus, and the Holy Spirit. How do I now incorporate the Holy Spirit in this relationship with God the Father and Jesus, my Savior and my Redeemer? In my natural thinking, it didn't compute as we tend to say. But as a hungry and curious new believer, the wise thing to do was to seek help. It seemed logical to me that this kind of clarity could come only from spiritual leadership. So, I sought clarity from leadership in the Body of Christ. Unfortunately for me, their answers confused me even more. I needed definitions and distinctions, and no one I went to could provide me with a good definition of who the third person in the Godhead was, let alone how He functioned. At least nothing they told me provided the clarity I sought. It was not until I started studying and meditating on the book of John and the Acts of the Apostles (especially Acts of the Apostles) that I began to understand who the Holy Spirit is and how He functioned in the lives of believers.

I first encountered the person of the Holy Spirit in the Scriptures in the Book of John. In John Chapter 14 while Jesus was preparing his disciples for His return to the Father He told them,

> *"I am going there to prepare a place for you. And if I go and prepare a place for you, If you love me, keep my commands.* [16] *And I will ask the Father, and he will give you another advocate to help you and be with you forever* [17] *the Spirit of truth. The world cannot accept him, because it neither sees him nor knows him. But you know him, for he lives with you and will be in you.* [18] *I will not leave you as orphans; I will come to you.* [19] *Before long, the world will not see me anymore, but you will see me. Because I live, you also will live.* [20] *On*

that day you will realize that I am in my Father, and you are in me, and I am in you."

Apart from assuring His disciples that He would not leave them comfortless, Jesus assured them that He would send them the Holy Spirit to be their advocate and to comfort them. He also explained to them that the Holy Spirit would play a critical role in their lives and in the lives of all believers by empowering them to do extraordinary things by exercising faith in His name.

> *"Very truly I tell you, whoever believes in me will do the works I have been doing, and they will do even greater things than these because I am going to the Father. [13] And I will do whatever you ask in my name, so that the Father may be glorified in the Son. [14] You may ask me for anything in my name, and I will do it."*

Among the many important roles the Holy Spirit would play in the life of the early disciples believers would be, first and foremost, to empower them to spread the good news of the Gospel of Jesus Christ to the ends of the earth. The Holy Spirit would empower them to clearly communicate all the things they learned from Jesus while He was yet with them on the earth. The second, and equally important role, Jesus assured His disciples in John 17 that the Holy Spirit would play, not only in their lives, but in the lives of all believers was a unifying one. Through His indwelling presence, the Holy Spirit would collaborate with the Father and the Son to unify, not only the disciples, but all those who would come to believe in Jesus Christ as their Lord and Savior through their preaching of the Gospel message to the ends of the earth.

From studying these passages of Scripture, I realized that the Holy Spirit was a completely different entity in the Godhead. He is not Jesus, and He is not the Father; in essence, He has a different function from Jesus and the Father. Two of His most important functions are to reveal

Jesus to every Christian and remind them of everything Jesus taught (John 14:15-20). These accounts in the scriptures of who the Holy Spirit is and what His roles and responsibilities are in the body of Christ made more sense to me than what the authority figures in the church were attempting to explain to me.

In John Chapter 17, I encountered a very important prayer. It is a prayer where Jesus was praying with all His heart for His disciples and for those who would believe in Him after He returned to His Father. He prayed for something that caught my attention. He acknowledged an existing unity in the Godhead, that is among the Father, the Son and the Holy Spirit, and went on to ask the Father for the same unity to exist among his disciples and be extended to all believers in Christ Jesus today. He prayed,

> *"I am praying not only for these disciples but also for all who will ever believe in me through their message. I pray that they will all be one, just as you and I are one as you are in me, Father, and I am in you. And may they be in us so that the world will believe you sent me. May they experience such perfect unity that the world will know that you sent me and that you love them as much as you love me. Father, I want these whom you have given me to be with me where I am. Then they can see all the glory you gave me because you loved me even before the world began."* (John 17:20-24 NLT).

The Holy Spirit is not only the presence of God in our lives, empowering us to do all that God has called us to do and become all that God has called us to be; He is also a peacemaker. Although Jesus did not mention the unifying role of the Holy Spirit, various other passages of scripture confirm that His presence is needed to unify us so that the world will know that Jesus Christ is the promised Savior. While Jesus the Christ or the Anointed One was charged with the redemptive role by his death and resurrection to redeem mankind to God, one of the most important roles of the Holy Spirit is to bring unity or peace among God the Father, Jesus, and all believers.

We can never accomplish peace with God except through the power of the Holy Spirit working within us. God, Himself says it is not by human might or power that we accomplish anything on this earth; it is only by the power of the Holy Spirit. God designed it that way so that we can see the perfect unity in the Godhead. God is the author of our salvation, Jesus completed the plan of God as Savior, and the Holy Spirit opens up the eyes of our understanding so that only through divine revelation occasioned only by Him can we come to experience the fullness of the Godhead. We will return to the many roles and functions of the Holy Spirit later in the book and how we can partner with Him to experience His amazing power in our lives.

Years ago, when God began to open the eyes of my understanding to the preceding, I was convinced that I couldn't function effectively without receiving this special gift of empowerment, the Holy Spirit. It was then that I prayed to receive Him, and God heard my prayer, and I received the baptism of the Holy Spirit with the evidence of speaking in unknown tongues. It was around that time while dealing with life challenges and adversities, I began to hear a voice within me giving me clear instructions when I needed them, encouragement when I was discouraged, strength when I was weak, and joy in times of sorrow. I was still not sure whose voice I was hearing, but as I continued to study the person of the Holy Spirit and to develop a closer relationship with Him, I began to realize that the voice I was hearing and the person working within me was actually not Jesus, but it was the Holy Spirit of God.

By now, you're probably having a similar reaction to what I discovered. You may be confused, but I don't want you to worry about how this all works just yet. I am going to walk you through a complete understanding of this throughout this book. Are you ready to experience that amazing abundant life in the Spirit that is the promise of the Father to each of us as believers? If you are, I want you to fasten your spiritual and mental seatbelts as we explore this topic together.

Many books have been written about the Holy Spirit, and we have benefited from the works of the men and women who dedicated time to studying and writing about Him. This book was written to provide you with working knowledge and a practical application of the inner workings of the Holy Spirit. I felt compelled to share this knowledge with you, my fellow believers, to implore you to receive the Holy Spirit. I want you to be empowered to bring glory to God and have an intimate relationship with Him. Only then will you come to an understanding that without Him, there is no way you will be able to live your life from the inside out and experience the abundant life Christ came to guarantee that we have.

As I engage you and enlighten you on the person of the Holy Spirit, allow me to also introduce Him to you as your Divine Coach. We will be diving deeply into the subject, and after our journey together, you will fully understand how important He is in helping you attain the life God has predestined for you, one that allows you to live your life from the inside out.

INTRODUCTION

This book will explore the various challenges and adversities we face or have faced in life and our corresponding responses or reactions to those challenges. I was motivated to write this book because I have been through many challenges and transitions in my life, and I noticed that my perception of these challenges has transformed and continues to transform me into the best version of myself. I have also met many people who shared with me the challenges they have encountered in their lives, and their experiences have been similar – they were transformed into the best version of themselves when they thought through the challenges and adversities they faced. Others have had different outcomes by reacting to those challenges and adversities instead of responding to them. It is important to remember that life doesn't just happen to us; we have the responsibility and the ability within to choose. We can choose to either respond or choose to react. Our response or reaction will result in the outcome and the quality of life we ultimately experience.

This book is also about the inner voice, which is your belief system, and the role that inner voice plays in your life events. It will teach you how to examine and overrule, if necessary, the belief system you originally inherited from those well-meaning authority figures that were present in your life. In order to have the results and the life you want, you need to be listening to another voice, the inner voice of your Divine Coach that was gifted to you at your divine rebirth.

In this book, I present a series of life-challenging situations that I faced and how they transformed my life. I also share some challenging situations that some familiar Biblical characters, some contemporary people you may be familiar with, and some famous and not so famous people experienced in their lives. Based on their unique perspective or evaluation of these situations, I discuss their responses or reactions to those challenging situations.

You will see from our life challenging experiences whether we were guided in our choices and decision making, who guided us in making those choices, and, based on our unique perspectives, what the outcome of our responses or reactions were. You will hear from our stories what place divine guidance had in our responses and what place our emotions had in our reactions. From our stories, you will be able to determine what impact the challenges had on our lives and how our responses or reactions impacted our lives.

Undoubtedly, you have heard the saying, as a man *or woman* thinks in his or *her* heart, so is he or *she* (gender addition and italics are mine). Now, where does our thinking come from? Our thinking originates from our belief system or our faith which is stored in our subconscious mind. I liken the subconscious mind to the inner voice within. We have all been gifted with an inner voice. This inner voice generated from our belief system is often called the subconscious mind, wherein our emotions and will lie. That inner voice develops as we grow into consciousness.

Our belief systems are socially and environmentally formed and nurtured. They remain dormant and form part of our unconscious until we have reason to access them later in life. When faced with life situations, they surface unconsciously. We then proceed to apply them unconsciously without questioning their validity and relevance, whether they serve us, how they serve us, and what the outcome would be if we apply those belief systems to our particular life situations. If left unquestioned, our belief system becomes the thinking or the perspective we bring to bear on all our life experiences, including our challenges and adversities. The thinking we bring to our life situations translates into our actions and behaviors and becomes our results and life outcomes. Our life outcomes are directly correlated with our belief systems which lie in our subconscious minds; that is why it is said that as we think, so we are. It simply means that we are responsible for our results. And unless we think about our results and change our behaviors and actions so that we get the results we want, we will continue to unconsciously act and wonder why we are receiving the outcomes that we do not want.

Apart from your belief system, your conscious and subconscious mind are generally referred to as your intuition which we will discuss further in the book. Additionally, this book is intended to support you in maximizing your life's potential by raising your awareness not only to the powerful role of the Divine Coach within but to help you raise your awareness of the powerful role your belief systems, your thoughts, and imagination have in you accessing the abundant life you desire. I guarantee you that if you examine your belief system and you become aware of the belief system on which your thinking is based, and you go a step further and change your belief system and your thinking to correspond with the kind of life you want, then you can have the life you want. Why do I make this bold statement? Because the quality of life you have right now is a result of your belief system, the level of your consciousness, and the quality of thinking you bring to your life. In other words, the life you have now resulted from your perception of the challenges and adversities you faced in life. And your life perception is informed by your belief system, which is the level of consciousness you employ in your choices and decision-making.

Please note that it is not my intention to address the topic of consciousness in this book. But just to present a bit of clarification as to what I am referring to as consciousness here. It is not a bunch of thoughts or a level of understanding. We have different aspects or dimensions of intelligence functioning within us; our body and cellular structure have their own intelligence. There is a conscious level of intelligence that is discerning in nature. There is emotional intelligence and genetic intelligence, and all of these intelligences are ruled by memory, but consciousness is not memory or being awake or alert. In fact, consciousness is not of the mind either.

Consciousness is a dimension of intelligence that is free from memory; it is boundless. Suffice it to say that your consciousness is still on whether you are awake or not. You are always available to consciousness whether you are asleep or awake; you cannot escape it. The question is whether it is available to you. As you will see from the story that follows, this consciousness was available to this old man.

CHAPTER I

Challenges or Opportunities: Maybe, Maybe Not

Life's challenges are life's opportunities presented to you in the form of challenges, and how you approach these challenges is critical to your life results.

Some years ago, in a leadership group coaching session, our leadership coach told us a very compelling story of an old man who lived in a village with his only son which I will share with you with the hope that it will impact you as it impacted me by changing my perspective regarding how I viewed life challenges and adversities.

One day, the old man and his son went hunting in the forest. As was customary, they parted ways for a while, but, alas, when the old man was ready to return home, the son was nowhere to be found. When the old man returned home to the village, he told the villagers what had happened. Naturally, the villagers were very sad. They lamented, "Oh what bad luck!" "What a terrible thing to have happened to your son." The old man responded, "Well, maybe, maybe not."

A few days later, the young man returned to the village with many horses. Now, horses represented great wealth in this village. Naturally, the villagers were quite overjoyed at the good fortune of the old man and his son. They exclaimed, "How wonderful! We are so happy for you, old man. First, your son got lost. Now, he is back with great wealth. What good luck! What great fortune!" The old man responded again, "Well, maybe, maybe not."

Immediately, the young man took to training the horses which he eventually sold, keeping one of the horses for himself. Sometime later, he went out riding. The horse threw him off, and he fell and broke his leg. He returned home to the village with his broken leg. The villagers again lamented the bad luck of the old man and his poor son. Their reaction was the same as before. "Oh, what bad luck!" "What a terrible thing to have happened to you and your son." The old man's response was the same as before, "Well, maybe, maybe not."

Sometime later, the country in which the old man and his son lived was at war, and the army needed to recruit all the able-bodied young men for the war. When they couldn't find enough able-bodied men in the city, the recruiters had no choice but to recruit from all the surrounding towns and villages. Yes, you guessed right. They came to the village where the old man and his son lived. They called for all the able-bodied men in the village, men who were young and strong with no physical defects. Men fit for fighting. For the villagers, being allowed to defend their country was an honorable thing. And, as much as the old man's son wanted to defend his country, he could not be recruited because he had just gotten his leg broken from his fall. You guessed right again. The villagers' reaction again was the same. They lamented, "Oh, what bad luck." "Oh, how terrible. Now, your son cannot take part in such an honorable war to defend our country because of his broken leg. Oh, how awful! What bad fortune that has befallen you and your son." You guessed right again. The old man's response was the same as before, "Well, maybe, maybe not."

As you read this account of the old man and his son and the events that occurred in their lives, I imagine that some of the challenges you have faced or are currently facing in your own life came to mind. You may have experienced painful losses in your life – you may have lost your job and are trying to find one, you may have lost your home, you have undergone a painful divorce, you may have lost a loved one in death, your credit may have been ruined because of medical bills, or a host of other life circumstances beyond your control. We all go through life challenges in life. We cannot escape them. But we do not all view them in the same way. Based on our perspective, we will either respond or react to them and as a result, we will have very different outcomes.

Life Challenges and Our Perspectives

For the purposes of this book, I will define perspective as our unique perception. It is what we see when we look through our personal magnifying glasses or lenses. The inner eye is how we perceive the events or challenges that come into our lives. Therefore, our perspective is how we view, evaluate, assess, or think about a life event, a life experience, or a life challenge.

In ocular science, our perception could be defined as a certain technique or process that could be used in aiding or correcting our vision. In this process, a glass is used to magnify or amplify an object to give the illusion of depth and distance, and, in this way, our naked eye receives more light. As a result of that added light, we are able to see more than we would ordinarily see without the use of this magnifying glass. Someone like me, for example, diagnosed with astigmatism where my distance vision is impaired, sees more clearly with the help of prescription glasses to aid my vision. Without the aid of these corrective lenses, what I see in the distance would be different from what someone without astigmatism would see. The lens through which we view a challenge ahead of us in life would give each of us a different perception and thus a different response.

Everyone has a unique perspective when faced with a life event; it is our interpretation, opinion, or belief. Our perspective or perception leads to our unique thought patterns. Thought patterns are a series of thoughts that cross our minds when faced with life events that almost always require us to do something; that is, they need us to respond. These thoughts are compelling because they produce emotions or feelings. Yes, our thoughts influence the way we feel about the events in our lives, and we respond or react based on those feelings.

The way we feel about what is going on in any challenging life event could lead us to respond appropriately or react inappropriately. As a result of our unique perspective about that life challenge, and the corresponding feeling associated with our unique view or perspective of that life challenge, we will either choose to respond or react. Your response or reaction resulting from that feeling automatically leads you to an outcome. Do you know that where you are today in your life and the quality of life you have right now is directly correlated with your perspective or the way you think about things? It's true. The way you think about life impacts your feelings, your feelings affect your decisions, and your decisions produce the life you have today. Reflect on this for a moment.

I want you to examine your perspective on any of the life challenges you are facing today. Allow me to suggest that your response will determine not only how you interact with this book but, more importantly, how you approach life and the kind of life you have right now. You see, your perspective about life challenges reveals a lot about you.

The Holy Scriptures challenge us to welcome life adversities and challenges as friends, suggesting that they are necessary for our personal growth and development. Here is how James puts it, "Consider it pure joy, my brothers and sisters, whenever you face trials of many kinds, because you know that the testing of your faith produces perseverance. Let perseverance finish its work so that you may be mature and complete, not lacking anything." (James 1:2-3 NIV)

At the same time, though, the Scriptures also warn us that we should be mindful of our thoughts and perceptions. Our perspective has a lot to do with the quality of thinking we bring to life challenges and adversities. Here is what the Scriptures say, "As a man thinks in his heart, so is he." (Proverbs 23:7 NKJV). In other words, our life experiences directly correlate with how we think and what we think about. This suggests that our thoughts are so powerful that they bring about our life reality.

As you go further into this book and read about my life experiences and the experiences of others presented, I invite you to consider your pattern in dealing with your life challenges and the usual outcome. If from your reflections, you determine that your perspective and your corresponding reaction do not serve you and that the outcome you usually get is not what you hoped for, then I would like to suggest, or even challenge you to change your perspective, shift your paradigm, change your mental model, and be more intentional in bringing about the outcome you want in your life. If you do, I guarantee that you will have the life you want. You will begin to experience the abundance and the freedom you always desired in your life. You will begin to expand your capacity and experience incredible abundance in every dimension of your life: spiritual, personal, physical, emotional, relational, financial, and professional. You will experience what I describe as maximum potential living, and this is what you want, isn't it? You want to maximize your life potential. Don't you? Yes, you do, but you won't be able to experience maximum potential living unless you raise your awareness of whether you respond or react to life challenges and adversities.

Challenges Versus Adversity Defined

What exactly is the difference between a life challenge and life adversity? Many people tend to use them interchangeably. However, a challenge is very different from an adversity; they are not the same. As defined by the dictionary, a challenge is synonymous "with a call to take part in a contest or a competition, especially a duel."[1] In essence, you could view a challenge as being in a contest or a fight; more than likely, a challenge is some life situation that requires great mental or physical effort to be completed successfully and therefore tests a person's ability. If you are faced

---

[1] "Challenge Definition & Meaning," Lexico
https://www.lexico.com/en/definition/challenge, (accessed 11/30/21)

with a challenge, it is more than likely someone or something is making life difficult for you.

There are several antonyms or opposites to the word challenge – they are to accept, embrace, or endure. When faced with a challenge, we can see that challenge as a being in a contest or a fight. That is, we can view the challenge as a situation that is in direct opposition to us. If that is the case, it is only natural that we will want to defend ourselves or fight it. If, however, we were to look at the opposite of the word, we could choose to accept, embrace, or endure the challenge. It all depends on our perspective, whether we choose to view the challenge at first glance as something we ought to fight; this is the obvious reaction. Or, we can turn it on its head and do the opposite of what seems obvious and embrace the challenge as an opportunity to become the best version of ourselves. But I'm sure you will agree with me that embracing a challenge as an opportunity to become the best version is easier said than done.

The Merriam-Webster Dictionary defines adversity as "a state, condition, or instance of serious or continued difficulty, tragedy or misfortune."[2] I want to emphasize a subtle distinction between the two words for the purposes of this book. An adversity unlike a challenge is a difficult life event, that depending on the severity, could continue indefinitely. In some cases, you do not have any control over them. Take death, for example; you cannot choose to end it. You have absolutely no control over death; you have to embrace death when it comes, and the pain of it can continue indefinitely. A life challenge may continue for a time, but it does not have to continue depending on our perspective of that challenge and how we address it; we can choose to either embrace or end it.

Unlike the definition of adversity, the definition of a challenge seems to have a positive connotation. One could accept it, endure it or embrace it, while in the case of an adversity, it would seem unreasonable to ask anyone to embrace a difficulty, which continues indefinitely. It would be reasonable to expect someone facing adversity to put up a fight, to do their

2 "Adversity Definition & Meaning," Merriam Webster, https://www.merriam-webster.com/dictionary/adversity, (accessed 11/30/21)

best to prevent it from happening, oppose it, or combat it for the sake of survival. As human beings, we have a built-in survival instinct, and our natural response, when faced with adversity, is fight or flight. We never see adversities as good for us.

A life challenge could be good for you if you see it as an opportunity for growth and change. An adversity could be just what its name suggests, an adverse or oppressive life event that could have a serious negative outcome, depending on your perspective. Or perhaps you may say to me, maybe, maybe not. You might be one of those people who is like the old man at the beginning of this chapter who had a unique perspective or way of viewing the events that happened in his life. You may be able to see life events, not as either-or, but you see the value in both perspectives; maybe they are challenges and are opportunities as well. It all depends on whether you choose to respond or to react.

Now, perhaps you might be thinking, what is the difference between a response and a reaction anyway? These are good questions because that means I have managed to get you engaged quite early in the book, and this was exactly my intent. I would like you to think deeply as you read and respond to the questions I ask you throughout the book. I would like you to go deep inside and see how you have been engaging in life.

In the next section, I will provide you with some distinctions and differences about the concepts presented in this section to lay the groundwork for the rest of the book. I will explain from my vantage point the difference between a response and a reaction and a challenge and an adversity so that you will get the maximum benefit from reading this book. For now, just suffice it to say that a thoughtful response would most likely bring you the outcome you wanted from a life challenge, while a knee-jerk reaction could throw you into another challenging situation.

To live your life from the Inside out requires you to respond, not react to life challenges, adversities, changes, and transitions. The old man in the story mentioned above responded to his life challenges while the villagers reacted. We will be learning more about this as we get further into the book.

A Reaction Versus a Response

When presented with adversity or a life challenge, the natural initial reaction is to resist the challenge or the adversity and fight for your life. If you see the challenge as an opposing force against you, obviously, you would want to go into combat. You will not embrace it, and hardly would you be expected to accept it. When someone slaps you on the cheek, this person is challenging you into a fight, and the natural reaction would be to strike back even harder. Who has ever heard of turning the other cheek, as Jesus suggests? It is not the way of the world as you will be judged as weak. So, when faced with an adversity or a life challenge, our natural reaction would be to fight back or defend ourselves. The dominant culture expects us to react this way; anything less would be judged as weak.

On the contrary, when faced with a life challenge, to respond is to take the time to think it through. To respond is to analyze the situation and ask yourself what is the wisest decision to make or the best course of action to take? What are the consequences of not doing something different? How would my life and the lives of those connected to me be different when I take this action? What outcome do I want? The action you take will determine your outcome or your results. When you bring that level of analysis or thinking to each of your life challenges, you can be assured that you will have the kind of life you want in cases where you are the only one responsible for the outcome. Remember, the life you have right now results from the level of analysis or critical thinking you brought to bear on the challenges you are faced within your life. But, I must warn you that your response will depend not on what you want but who you are, that is, the level of your consciousness or your awareness of the voice of the Divine Coach within. That consciousness of who He is, your ability to hear His voice, and to follow His directions is what will inform your perspective, your thoughts, your actions, your outcomes, and ultimately the quality of life you have.

I believe that life's challenges are life's opportunities presented to you in the form of challenges, and how you approach these challenges is critical to your life results. Life is governed by a set of principles, and one of those is the Law of Cause and Effects or Results. That principle says that for every result or experienced life outcome, there is a cause. Extrapolating from this Law of Cause and Effects or Results, you can say that your belief system, which is the causal agent, determines your thoughts. Your emotionalized thoughts, that is the emotion you attach to your thoughts, determine your actions and your actions determine your results. To experience the life you want, let me encourage you to examine your thoughts and the emotions you attach to those thoughts before you make decisions or take any kind of action.

I want to challenge you to do a close introspection and reflect on your life. What has been your response to the challenges you faced in the past or those you currently face? Did you react, or are you reacting? Were you able to respond, or are you responding? What were your thoughts about your life challenges, and what emotions guided your response? For those of you who have gone through one or more life challenges, what was the outcome, and what was your response or reaction to the challenge? What outcome did you expect or desire? If I were to ask you who or what guided your response or your reaction to the challenge, what or who would you say guided you or is guiding you? Could you attribute part of your response to that challenge to a counselor, a life leadership or business coach, a psychologist, a therapist, or a spiritual guide?

Perhaps it was a dear friend who supported you, or maybe a book you read provided you with the response you needed or led you to make the choice you eventually made. Some of you may tell me that your response was guided by your gut feeling, your intuition, or some inner voice. Maybe you could point to prayer or deep meditation. Perhaps you were inspired by the emotions of love, joy, peace, patience, faithfulness, gentleness, goodness, kindness, or self-control. You might have been guided by your moral values or your belief system. Others of you might say, "my reaction to this life challenge was driven by fear, immense fear." In that crucial decision-making moment, some of you may have experienced one of these emotions: insecurity, doubt, frustration, impatience, anger, jealousy, or pride. For some of you, perhaps, it was even a long-standing behavioral pattern of self-indulgence. You may have indulged in some form of substance abuse, drugs, alcohol, or food that was not checked at the inception, and it has now become a habit that is difficult to overcome. Now, you find that you are on autopilot, and all the choices you make are unexamined. Then one day, you realize that you are not where you want to be, and you ask yourself, *How did I get here? Where did I go wrong? What can I do to change the results I am having?*

These are some of the hard questions everyone must address in their life. Though these questions may seem daunting, they must be addressed if you want to experience abundance, peace, success, and prosperity. But, don't worry, throughout this book, I will provide you with the tools, principles, and strategies you need to shift your life into alignment with the Divine Coach. As you dive further into the understanding of how His influence in your life will affect your life choices, you will realize that you've most likely been taking the hard route. If you are willing to submit to the Divine Coach within, you will find there is an abundant life waiting for you.

CHAPTER II

The Principles of Intentional Living

Life Doesn't Give You What You Want. Life Gives You Who You Are.

As we go through the seasons of our lives, I am aware that we will all have numerous life transition experiences. Despite the myriad of changes, challenges, and adversities that we all must experience, you and I must be intentional about living the abundant life Christ promised us. Yet, despite the guarantees Christ gave us, it is up to us to ensure that we intentionally cooperate with Jesus by doing our part. We must do our part to have that abundant, fulfilled life.

I want to challenge you to go within and respond to three very critical questions that are necessary for accessing your potential.

1. How far are you willing to go to have that life of significance you are dreaming of living?
2. What sacrifices are you willing to make to access your unlimited potential so that you can have that life of fulfillment and significance that you desire?

3. What are the limiting beliefs standing in the way of expanding your potential to live a life of fulfillment and significance?

Take some time to meditate on these questions because if you are willing to commit to intentional living, you must also be committed to stretching yourself beyond your comfort zone by placing yourself in environments and situations with people who are also intentional.

The Principles of Intentional Living

Living intentionally will give you the life you want. Intentional living is the only way to experience maximum potential living and become the best version of yourself. Intentional living will require you to grow and expand your capacity in every dimension of your life, that is, in the physical, emotional, relational, spiritual, and financial dimensions. It will require you to leave the realm of the superficial and the external and take a deeper dive into the realm of the spiritual. It will require that you go within to discover the unlimited potential God has given you to live the abundant life that you desire. Let me ask you, do you want the life you have right now? What kind of life do you envision for yourself and your loved ones? Make no mistake, to have the life you want, you must be intentional. You must be willing to examine who you are, where you are right now, and where you want to go. You must be willing to challenge your belief system, and you must examine what you know and what you do to see if they align. If they don't, then you must be courageous enough to go through a process of unlearning. If you do not have the life you want, set aside what you know to learn some new things. I would even go a bit further to challenge you to change your mindset; you must be willing to change your thinking, evaluate your values, and ask yourself the questions, *Am I living by my values*? In other words, you must go within because in order to have the life you want, you must go within yourself. If you fail to go within, you will go without. It is this granular process of self-evaluation, one which examines your belief system, your emotionalized thoughts, values, and corresponding actions combined with the willingness to make the behavior changes that are aligned with your values that constitute intentional living.

Let me ask you to consider these powerful intentional living and life transformation principles:

Principle #1: Life doesn't give you what you want. Life gives you who you are.

Simply put, who you are and your current life is directly correlated to how and what you think. The Scriptures support this principle as seen in Proverbs 23:7: "For as he thinketh in his heart, so is he: Eat and drink, saith he to thee; but his heart is not with thee." Essentially, life will never take you further than the level of your consciousness or the level of your thinking. You will have to change your thinking for you to have the life you want. In other words, if you change your thinking, you will change your life. You will not be able to get out of life what you did not bring into it. The simple truth is that life sometimes doesn't give you what you think you want, not because you do not deserve it but because you really deserve more and do not know it. Change your thinking, and you will change your life outcomes. You do this by accessing the unlimited power and potential you have within.

Principle #2: The answer to all your life's challenges lies within you.

Intentional living requires you to become aware of your unlimited personal potential. Do you believe that you have unlimited potential? You see, for you to live a life of intentionality, you must first accept the fact that you have unlimited potential within you, which allows you to respond to all of life's challenges. We have all been gifted with everything we need to live a maximum potential life. Here is what the Scriptures have to say in support of this: "For His divine power has bestowed on us [absolutely] everything necessary for [a dynamic spiritual] life and godliness, through true and personal knowledge of Him who called us by His own glory and excellence." (2 Peter 1:3 AMP).

Principle #3: And, if you fail to go within, you will go without.

Each of us has been blessed with unlimited potential. The problem is that many people are not aware of this and that potential remains untapped simply because they lack this awareness; this is a dangerous state to live in. There are two reasons why I say this is a dangerous state to live in. First, if that potential is left untapped, you will rob others of the value that only you can add to them. Second, you are the co-creator of your life; in fact, you created the life you have right now. It was not luck or chance; you designed the life you currently have. Intentional living requires that we go within to access the unlimited potential we have been gifted with to experience maximum potential living. To expand your resilience capacity, you must be willing and intentional to go within to access the unlimited potential you have been gifted, or else you will be living life beneath your potential, listening to limiting beliefs that will feed you all the reasons why you do not have the life you want. Usually, it will be someone or something outside of you and not you. If you fail to go within, you will look at your life and compare it with the life others around you have and attribute it to luck. This calls for letting go of the things you know and going within for the answers which your spirit knows better than your external environment.

Principle 4: Intentional living requires that you go within to expand your resilience capacity.

Intentional living requires our willingness to grow and expand our resilience capacity. You may be asking, *well, how do I do that?* You do so by leveraging the changes, challenges, and adversities that life transition experiences bring you. If this idea seems a bit foreign to you or if you admit you have been struggling in this area, I promise you that you will develop your resilience by the time you have finished reading this book.

Before we move on any further, I invite you to reflect on the following questions below to receive the maximum benefit from the section you have just read.

1. How far are you willing to go to live an intentional life?
2. What sacrifices are you willing to make to live that intentional life?
3. What are the limiting beliefs standing in the way of you living an intentional life?

To live that intentional life, you must reflect on yourself and where you are in your life. You must be longing to do something significant and make a contribution to do something noble and purposeful. So where do you start? First, you start with knowing yourself. Second, you go on to growing yourself. Third you proceed to add value to others. Then, you move on from adding value to others to adding value with others. Finally, you move on from adding value with others to living a life of significance.

Living a Life of Significance:

Do you believe you can a life of significance? What is significance? Let me tell you what significance isn't. It does not mean you have to be rich and famous. It doesn't mean you have to accomplish anything. To be significant all you have to do is make a difference wherever you can and with whatever you have.

In his book, Intentional Living, John Maxwell says, "The world is a dangerous place not because of those who do evil but because of those who look on and do nothing." In these challenging times we live in, you and I can do a lot to make this world a better place; it takes only one person to start. You don't have to do it all. All you have to do is to identify one need in the world and start, and you will see how many will join your movement. Making this world a better place calls for intentionality.

To be significant all you have to do is to make a difference wherever you are. One person can act and make a change that will inspire another person to be intentional, and those people can partner with each other and start a movement. It takes one person to start that movement and that person can be you. And, who knows, according to Esther 4:4 you may have been chosen to add value to the lives of those you come in contact with right where you are now, in your environment in the Kingdom for just such a time as this.

Living a life of significance simply means you must be intentional about making a difference with whatever you have, however you can, and doing it right now. The truth is that whatever you have, your unique skills, abilities, perspectives and talents are more than enough to begin making a difference in your world. All you need is the belief that fuels action and the willingness to start small, where you are and with what you have. Once you begin, you will find that you can make a significant difference that will add massive value in the world.

CHAPTER III

Live Your Life From the Inside Out: What Do You Believe?

"As a man thinketh in his heart, so is he..."

Proverbs 23:7

To live your life from the inside out, you must challenge your belief system, renew your mind, expand your personal capacity and develop the resilience to respond to life challenges so that you can have the amazing abundant life you were destined to have. To support you in doing that, in this chapter, I will discuss your belief system, how it was formed and why it is critical to examine your current belief system if you want to experience the life you desire. I hope to raise your awareness that you are the co-creator of the life you have. You made specific decisions that brought you to the place you are. Life will present you with particular challenges and adversities, and daily you are reacting or responding to those challenges whether you realize it or not. My desire as you read is to raise your awareness of what I call the performance gap, that is, the gap between what you say you believe and what you are actually doing, and to help you close that performance gap. My desire for you is that you begin the process of taking control of your life and start making courageous changes so that you can enjoy the life of success and significance you want for yourself and your loved ones instead of living life on autopilot where you have to constantly and unconsciously change things you don't want. I want you to align your belief and values with your life calling and fulfill that divine calling upon your life courageously; this is the action I had to take. One day, I had to be very sincere with myself, and I had to reflect on my life and ask myself, *is the life I have the one I want? If not, what life do I want for my only son that God blessed me with? What do I have to give, and who do I want to add value to besides my son? What sacrifices am I willing to make to have the life I want for my son and me?* That reflection led me to challenge my belief system, and in doing so, work on leveraging the challenges I was facing and then to develop the resilience to courageously fulfill my divine calling.

Challenging My Belief System to Develop Resilient Faith: My Story

As I reflect on my life, I realize that along life's difficult journey, my faith in God and my belief system, my grandmother's mentoring, and a good basic education contributed to my resilient responses to life challenges and adversities. Had it not been for that resilient faith, I would not have been able to endure the adversities and respond to life challenges in the way I did. Allow me to explain this more in-depth.

In 2007, I began to feel that stirring in my heart that I had reached a peak point in my life. I was feeling dissatisfied and couldn't determine why I was so miserable. I later realized that I had drifted from my life purpose and was concentrating on making money instead of seeking fulfillment. I had retired from my corporate job and decided that I would get into real estate. Sales were totally out of my league, but I decided to give it a try. This was definitely not what I was called to do, and I knew it. So, I discussed it with my husband, and we agreed that I would leave the real estate industry and return to my life calling and purpose and, the love of my life, a combination of mentoring and coaching for personal spiritual growth.

I committed our decision to God in prayer as I usually do with any major life decision. It was a huge transition, and I wanted to succeed. I committed to working with corporate leaders, helping them to maximize their potential and expand their personal and leadership influence. I remember vividly praying these words, "Lord, if there is anything or anyone standing in the way of me doing that, I give you permission to remove that thing or person out of my life." It was a commitment, and I meant it from the bottom of my heart, only I did not know what the outcome was going to be.

Two weeks later, on March 6, 2008, at 11:30 am, I heard a knock on my front door. I did not expect anyone, but my son who had previous knowledge of the visitors and why they were coming, let them in. They came to bring me the devastating news that my husband had lost his life in a tragic car accident in Tanzania, Africa. As he was used to doing for sixteen years, he traveled to Africa to continue working on a Social Assistance Fund Project that he managed for the international organization he worked for. He sacrificed his life working with the people he loved: widows, orphans, and vulnerable children in Africa.

This was the most painful news I had ever received in my life. At that moment, I knew that if I gave in to the pain I was experiencing, I could quite possibly die from grief. I am a woman of great faith with the conviction that everything that happened to me in this life was directed by God. I brought every life experience, whether good or bad, to God in prayer, and this is what I did at that time; I immediately went to my prayer closet. My prayer closet is a special place in my home that I have dedicated to prayer, and it is there that I prayed for God to strengthen and help me. As I prayed on my knees, I specifically remember hearing that familiar voice of the Holy Spirit of God saying to me, "Worship Me," and I immediately began to worship God. I recalled how good God had been to me over the years and as I recalled his goodness, faithfulness, provision, direction, and most of all His amazing love for me, which He demonstrated over the years, I thanked Him. I praised Him for His tremendous power to strengthen me and help me through this adversity.

I recalled growing up with my grandmother that she never complained when she was faced with a life challenge or an adversity. She was always on her knees praying, just as I was doing. I started praising God for His mighty power, His deliverance, and His ability to help me fight that spiritual battle. I didn't say, "God, why did you take my husband from me, and how could you allow that to happen to me?" No, instead, I remember committing the rest of my life in God's hands for Him to care for me.

While I was on my knees, my inspiration was Job from the Old Testament. I was inspired by this man who had lost all he had, including the children he loved, yet he retained his integrity. This man of resilient faith experienced great physical, emotional, spiritual, relational, and financial challenges. I cried out to the Lord as the pain of the loss sank in, "Though you slay me," and I added, "I know you won't slay me, I will continue to put my trust in you." I vowed to live a life of faith, commitment, and surrender to God for the rest of my life; I promised to do whatever He asked me to do.

At that moment, I felt an amazing sensation which I describe as a lightning bolt or great heat in the middle of my head warming me. The warmth traveled down to my neck and then to my shoulders, and finally, it made its way to my chest cavity and settled in my heart. Then, I heard the comforting voice of the Holy Spirit saying to me, "You are ready now to face this challenge. Get up." I had heard this voice so many times before that I had become familiar with it. It was the assuring voice of the Holy Spirit, my Divine Coach, encouraging me and assuring me that He was there with me and that I should not fear.

I experienced a great surge of inner peace and strength. I describe it as a special supernatural strength sent from God above to strengthen me in that time of deep grief and emotional pain and to empower me to face that life adversity. From that moment, I received a divine strength that I had never experienced before, and that has never left me. You can say that I received the gift of resilience or faith. I received inner strength, confidence, and resolve to carry on. I vowed not to let the pain I was experiencing stand in the way of me being strong for myself, my family, and my friends.

It has been thirteen years since my husband passed away. The agreement we made was that I would live out my life calling and purpose. We realized that my life purpose was to coach, mentor, and write. I agreed that I would write about the impact my grandmother had on mentoring and coaching me into becoming the resilient black woman I am today. Since then, I have dedicated myself to honoring the commitment I made to God and to my husband: to live a faith-filled life focused on my calling and aligning that calling with my Christian values. I help resilient Kingdom women of color in leadership to access their inner resilience to courageously live their life calling, values, and purpose.

I viewed the tragic death of my husband as a contribution to making me the best version of myself I could be. His death also provided a wonderful opportunity for my family and me to continue to make a difference in the lives of orphans and vulnerable youths in Africa, Latin America, the Caribbean, and here in the USA. Zorbas Orphans Fund, founded in December 2009, one year after my husband passed away, was not born because of this adversity it was despite the adversity. It was because of my belief system, the faith, and the resilience with which I was raised.

You see, my grandmother raised me to live my life from the inside out. She raised me with the belief system that the answer to life's challenges and adversities is within, not outside. I have dedicated my life to accessing the voice of the Divine Coach within and partnering with Him to live the life of my dreams. Today, I teach that our belief system and its impact on our response to life challenges and adversities determine if we are living our lives from the inside out. If you would like to experience a life of abundance and add value to the lives of others, it requires resilient faith, which must be based on a belief system centered on Godly principles and values.

What is Your Belief System?

What comes to your mind when you hear the words belief system? What exactly is a belief system? Do you know where your belief system originates from? Is your belief system the same as your faith? These are very important questions which I would like you to ponder on. Your belief system is an ideology that helps us to interpret our everyday reality. This belief system could be religion, political affiliation, philosophy, or spirituality, among many other things. These beliefs are shaped and influenced by different factors. For example, do you believe that the Bible is the Word of God? When it comes to human nature, do you believe that we are inherently good or inherently bad? Each of us has a core belief system that centers around the various dimensions of our life. For example, we have core beliefs about God, politics, religion, money, sex, gender (the rights of men and women), race, singleness, marriage, widowhood, raising children, nationality, education, immigration, budgeting, saving, investing, work retirement, values, leadership, goodness, giving, forgiveness, love, aging, death, etc. These beliefs are how we make sense of the world around us. Your belief system informs your thoughts.

It does not matter if our challenges are personal, physical, financial, relational, spiritual, professional, or emotional, our belief systems are at the root of every challenge. When we face challenges in any of those domains in our lives, we will either react, or we will respond to them. Our responses or reactions come from our belief system, which informs our mindset. Our life challenges will test our beliefs. This is why you must know first what you believe and, secondly, where your belief system comes from. Thirdly, you must identify how your belief system informs the way you respond to your life challenges.

For instance, if someone I would call, Anne, grew up in a household where her parents taught her that savings and investing are critical for success and peace of mind, that message would have impacted her financial belief system. Later in life, if Anne was faced with the loss of her job that she had for twenty years and she was the main income earner in her home, more than likely, she would have had a healthy savings or investment account or both. Anne's belief system would have contributed to her having an investment mindset. That belief system would undoubtedly have come from messages she received when growing up. She may have been told that she should always save for a rainy day, such that when she became an adult and started working, she would have adopted a savings money blueprint. Therefore, when Anne lost that job, her response would have been different from the reaction of the person who I will call Robert who grew up in a household whose money blueprint was not one of savings or investing.

Robert grew up in an environment where there was never enough to save but just enough to last until the next paycheck came. His money blueprint would be different from Anne's. Saving was never mentioned in his household, and unless he adapted the money blueprint of saving and investing later in life, it is more than likely that he would have adopted the mindset and behavior of the authority figures in his life when it comes to savings and investment. He would have a scarcity mindset. With that mindset, when Robert lost a job, his reaction would be one of fear, worry, and insecurity. While Anne would have chosen to save and invest, Robert would have chosen not to do so. When Robert and Anne became adults, their background socialization would play a major role in their financial behavior and life choices.

In responding to life's challenges, our belief system informs our mindset and money blueprint and plays a very important role in our life choices and financial behavior as well. You and I respond to life's challenges and adversities based on our awareness which informs the level of thinking we bring to life's challenges or adversities Anne and Robert responded or reacted differently to their financial challenges based on their level of awareness and thinking. In Anne's case, her parents raised her awareness that there was value in investing and saving for lean and difficult years, and thus her financial behavior, when she lost her job, manifested that she reached that level of understanding. In Robert's case, there was no awareness raised around the value of saving or investing such that during the years of financial difficulty, his response was different from Anne's. Anne was aware and prepared for the challenge and responded in confidence. Robert was unaware, and thus he was totally unprepared for the challenge, so he reacted in fear, insecurity, and worry. Anne's environment created an awareness, and Robert's environment created a blind spot.

Having a lack of awareness in any area of our lives is often referred to as having blind spots. Our belief system, which contributes to our awareness and blind spots, is often a product of background socialization and culture. We develop blind spots and preferences based on our belief system. In this section, we will discuss how your belief system contributes to your awareness, your blind spots, and your preferences.

In their book *Blindspot: Hidden Biases of Good People*,[3] Banji and Greenwald assert that our preferences—what and whom we like or dislike, favor or reject, nurture or thwart, approach or avoid can take different forms. They mention two systems that characterize the mind as discussed by psychologists for the purpose of building theories and conducting research. These two systems are the reflective and the automatic mind. From our example, the reflective or the conscious side of Robert's mind is not savings-friendly, and he can honestly say that there is nothing wrong with not concerning himself for the future when it comes to having a savings or investment account. Robert is a product of his background socialization, which includes his belief system, culture, and religion, where saving and investment were not valued. In some cultures, there is a religious belief system, misunderstood I might add from the scriptures, where money is believed to be the root of all evil and savings in whatever form is a demonstration of a lack of faith in God as the provider.

If Robert was brought up by parents with that religious belief then he would have internalized that belief system from his environment. Robert's subconscious mind would make this simple yet culturally potent association (money=root of evil=sin). Surely this will influence his thoughts, feelings, and behavior. Although Robert's conscious mind willingly accepts that

[3] Mahzarin R. Banagi; Anthony G. Greenwald, *"Blindspot: Hidden Biases of Good People,"* (New York, Delacorte Press, 2013)

there was nothing wrong with having money, the power of his subconscious mind (his belief system) would have controlled his behavior over the years. Finally, the thing he feared most, not having money, like a self-fulfilling prophecy, came upon him, and now his worst fears are realized. He lost his job, he did not save for the lean years, and he had no money to respond to his life's responsibilities and commitments.

We all have blind spots. Your blind spots are the areas of your life that others see and you don't. You have a public face which is how you communicate and interact with others. You also have a private face, which is how you communicate and behave when you are not under public scrutiny. There is also your default behavior, the way you react when you are under pressure. Finally, there is your self-perception which may not align with others' perception of you. So, let me ask you, have you considered what your blind spots are? Your faith, your values, and your belief system could play a huge role in your blind spots. Let us consider how they could contribute in the next section.

What is the Source of Your Belief System?

Our belief system is shaped and influenced by different factors. The knowledge of a certain topic, the way we were raised, for example, peer or social pressure are just some of the factors that contribute to or even can change our belief system. The convictions that come from those systems allow us to make sense of the world around us and our role within it.

Why is it important to know your belief system? Good question. Our belief systems affect our everyday lives and are commonly associated with religion. A religious belief system, for instance, is usually structured around the belief in one or more deities and the ability for supernatural occurrences to affect us and the universe that we exist in. A spiritual belief system is closely related to this but is not as structured. Some choose to believe in an afterlife and follow a moral code of conduct but do not choose to affiliate with any particular church or denomination.

Since a belief system affects how a person views the world and defines how they treat others, a spiritual belief system still counts as a belief system. Most of our belief systems and the way we perceive the world from the content of our subconscious mind come from our upbringing, our environment, peer pressure, and authority figures. When we were growing up, our caretakers passed on their convictions about life issues based on how they were raised and their personal life experiences, whether negative or positive. We, in turn, without question, accepted their convictions as our own, and they have become the lens through which we view the world around us.

As we interact with life and make choices and decisions, these learned environmental convictions or belief systems become our filters. In other words, our perception of the world, thoughts, feelings, and desires are colored by our belief system. We see everything through those conviction lenses, and they even become self-fulfilling prophecies. Why? Because human beings tend to select and see only that which line up with those convictions and ignore those that do not align with their beliefs. Instead of challenging those inherited convictions and allowing ourselves the luxury to use our free will and the power of choice to think differently about challenges, situations, and issues affecting our lives, we go along on autopilot and never question those belief systems that were passed on to us. They become our holy cows, as it were, and we resist any outside influences or challenges that will challenge us to think or believe differently lest we have to change. We are bent on not being influenced. We resist anyone or anything that will challenge us to think differently because we are afraid to change how we think and view the world. Then we wonder why we are not achieving the kind of success we desire out of life. To change our results or to change our life, we must challenge our belief system. We should ask ourselves, *do I really believe this?*

Though religion and spirituality are the most recognized forms of belief systems, there are several others like some of the ones I previously mentioned. Would you say that you align with the Democratic or the

Republican party? These political affiliations are what would be considered a political belief system.

A political belief system forms a person's political opinion about governments, their leaders, economic systems, and other social structures. For instance, how do you feel about topics such as immigration and health care, welfare, and paying taxes? What you think about these issues form your political belief system. Apart from religious, spiritual, and political belief systems, there are also racial, cultural, and geopolitical belief systems. It is important for us to know what our thoughts are about these, as well.

So, what or who would you say accounts for your religious, spiritual, political, cultural, racial, and geopolitical convictions? Are you aware of how they impact the choices and the outcome of your life? Belief systems are powerful in that they are responsible for the way we view the world. They form the basis for the choices you make and ultimately, the life you have now. Your faith, your thoughts, and your emotions derive from your belief system. This belief system has contributed to your decision-making and to your current life outcomes.

Your belief system, however, is not fixed. You have the ability to change it to where you can become the best version of yourself that you were created to be. If you recall, earlier in this chapter, I introduced you to this life principle: life doesn't give you what you want; life gives you who you are. And you become the best version of yourself only by accessing the divine potential that lies within you. Make no mistake, although you may think you can succeed in this life by depending on your belief system and your physical, mental, and emotional abilities, you cannot. You must go within to meet the only person who is able to help you live your life from the inside out, and that is the Holy Spirit of God.

The next chapter introduces you to the Divine Coach and how you can partner with Him to live your life from the inside out and have the life you want. You will be introduced to the amazing unlimited potential you have within you. You will discover how to access that unlimited potential that allows you to live your life to its fullest. This is the life each of us has been promised; it is the abundant life Jesus guaranteed He came to give to each believer, and it is the life I know that you have desired and have been seeking to find. It is life in the Spirit. But, first, I will make a distinction between who He is not and who He is so that you, as a believer, will not be confused as I was when I started my relationship with Jesus Christ.

CHAPTER IV

The Divine Coach: Who Is He?

"And I will pray the Father, and he shall give you another Comforter, that he may abide with you forever"

John 14:16,27 KJV

In the last few chapters, I explained the difference between living your life from the outside and living your life from the inside out. I discussed with you the impact of your external environment – and how those who had a role in nurturing you impacted your belief system. I also show how your imagination, thoughts, and faith correlate with your behavior and life outcomes. In essence, what I attempted to explain in the previous chapters is that your creator, God, for those of you who are of faith, has put within you His divine nature, and that divine nature has provided you with unlimited potential to become the best version of yourself and to enable you to have maximum life potential. That maximum potential life I define is a life of success, impact, and significance each of us was destined to have.

Sadly, many of you reading this book may not have that life of success and significance you desire. You strive without success. You desire to do more and to have more, and to become the best version of yourself. This striving for success could become frustrating, but you must remember that just because you want that life does not mean you will have that life. Life does not give you what you want; life will only give to you your authentic self, and, whether you're aware of it or not, life will always bring you a series of challenges located in the gap between where you are right now and where you want to be in the future. I further explained that if you are not satisfied with who you are today and your current life, your mind has to be renewed. You have to experience a transformational mindset. You renew your mind by changing who you listen to. You see, your external environment has had a big part to play in your current life outcomes. You may have been living your life from the outside in.

Before we move on, let me stop and ask you to reflect on these all-important questions. Who do you listen to? Whose voice do you listen to in order to make your life choices and your life decisions? Are you listening to the voices in your external environment to navigate through life? Who has been your guide helping you with your life decisions and your life choices? Are you listening to the voice the world describes as the sixth sense, the voice of your conscience, or the voice of your intuition? Most people will tell you that they listen to the voice of intuition. Let me explain what I mean.

The Voice of Intuition

Intuition is one of our most powerful and precious gifts in life. Some people call it a hunch, while others call it a gut feeling, sixth sense, the conscience, the voice of reason, and the inner voice. Indeed, we are all born with that voice within. That inner voice, which the scripture refers to as our conscience, provides each of us with the ability to distinguish between wrong and right and thus helps us in our decision-making process. When we are in touch with our intuition, we have greater self-awareness. We read situations, and we know the appropriate course of action intuitively to take in dealing with whatever life challenges we are facing at the time. In The *21 Irrefutable Laws of Leadership*, John Maxwell discusses the personal value and leadership relevancy of the gift of our intuition. According to him, intuition allows leaders to be great observers, readers of situations, trends, resources, and people. Most importantly, leaders become readers of themselves, their inner world, emotional states, weaknesses, strengths, and blind spots.[4]

When we are in tune with and listen to the inner voice of intuition, it never ceases to offer us, time and time again, a synthesis of much broader information than we can ever have access to from our intellect. Individuals with heightened intuitions can combine that internal information with previous experiences, insights, and perhaps with other unrelated experiences to draw conclusions.

Until we are born again of the Spirit of God and become aware of the role of the Divine Coach in our lives, our intuition forms the bedrock of the non-believer's potential to help respond to life's challenges. In that unenlightened spiritual state, intuition takes the place of the Divine Coach and should not be ignored. To ignore your intuitive ability is to ignore the higher intelligence within each of us before we become born again of the Spirit of God. That dependence on intuition, sixth sense, or gut feeling is the difference between an unbeliever and a believer in Jesus Christ, a person who is born again of the Holy Spirit of God. You are a tripartite being, body, soul, and spirit.

Many of you reading the book will become aware for the first time that you are not just a physical being but a tripartite being. You are made up of a physical body, but you have a soul and a spirit. Since you are familiar with your physical body, I won't spend any time on your physical body. I will dedicate this chapter to your soul and spirit and will make the distinction between your soul, your spirit, and the Holy Spirit, who I refer to as our Divine Coach.

---

[4] John C. Maxwell, *The 21 Irrefutable Law Of Leadership:Follow Them and People Will Follow You* (New York, HarperCollins Leadership, 2007)

What is the Soul?

"And the LORD God formed man of the dust of the ground, and breathed into his nostrils the breath of life; and man became a living soul"

(Genesis 2:7 KJV).

Genesis 2:7 KJV states, "And the Lord God formed man of the dust of the ground, and breathed into his nostrils the breath of life; and man became a living soul." This simply states that man was given a body, and God breathed into him the breath of life. It shows the fact that man's spirit comes from the Creator, whom we, people of faith, call God. When the Creator, God, breathed into the human being the breath of life, man became a living soul. This living soul speaks of man's consciousness. What does that mean? It means two things:

1. Man became conscious of his connection to the earth through his body and God, his Creator, through his soul.
2. Man became a thinking being with a will and emotions. By his own free will, man is capable of taking actions and making decisions independent of his Creator.

As an emotionalized being, man could feel and choose to make decisions based on his feelings or choose to make decisions directed by the Holy Spirit. However, to make decisions directed by the Holy Spirit, he must first be born again, be filled with the Holy Spirit, and develop a personal relationship with Him. We discuss this born-again experience in detail later on in the book.

The Creation of the Soul

According to the account of the creation in Genesis Chapter 2, man was created with two independent materials, spirit and body. When the spirit, or the breath of God, entered the body, the soul of man was produced. The soul is the result of the union of the spirit and the body. When the body was created from the earth, the body was dead, but when the breath of the Creator entered the body, a third independent entity was produced. That entity is the soul, which is a combination of the conscious mind and the subconscious mind; man became conscious and alive. In the conscious mind lies man's will, his power to make choices, his thoughts, the way he assesses, perceives, makes sense of his external environment and his emotions or feelings. Without the Spirit or the breath of God, which produced the soul of man, the body of man is dead; he is not conscious of his external environment. When the breath of God or God's spirit entered man's body, the body became alive. When a child is born, the spirit or the breath of God comes into that child's body, and something organic is produced. That something organic is the human soul or the human consciousness. When a man dies, the breath or his spirit leaves the body, and man loses all consciousness or life. Upon death, man has no thoughts, no will, and no emotions.

So, what do we conclude? Separate from the physical body formed out of the ground and the spirit of man that he received from the Spirit of his Creator, man also has a soul which is separate from his body and his spirit. That's why the scriptures say, "Man became a living soul." This signifies that the soul was created with that fusion or incorporation of the spirit and the body. So, both the spirit and the body are incorporated into the soul. In other words, the soul and the body are wholly joined to the spirit, and the spirit and the body are fully incorporated into the soul. This soul consists of the conscious mind and the subconscious mind. Through man's conscious mind, that is his five senses: he hears, sees, touches, smells, and tastes. It is through those five senses that man analyzes and makes sense of his external environment.

Man lives in a physical body that he uses to contact and communicate with his external environment, the outside world. In his book, *The Spiritual Man*, Watchman Nee explains it this way, "The soul is the consummation of the spirit and the body."[5] He goes on to say that when man was created, his soul was supposed to function like the chain linking the spirit and the body. The soul is the seat of man's personality. It is man's soul that makes it possible for him to exist independently. The soul is the totality of the elements within man; it is man's personality. The soul, of course, though it is a combination of spirit and body, is an independent element. In the same way, as the spirit and the body are two independent elements, the soul is an independent element. However, once the body and the spirit are joined together, the fusion of both creates a separate living entity, the soul.

The soul is an entity in which resides man's free will. Both the spirit and the body are incorporated into it; it has free will. If the soul chooses to obey God, it can make the spirit the master of everything as he is designed to function. But man can choose to suppress the spirit and take as its master the part it likes to obey. The three components of man, the spirit, the soul, and the body, is like a lighted electric bulb. Within the bulb, there is the electricity, the filament, and the light. The body, which is the physical part of man, is the filament. The spirit is the electricity, and the soul is the light. The electricity is the source of the light, and light is the consequence of the electricity. The filament is the physical material responsible for conducting the electricity and emitting light. When the spirit and the body combine, they produce the soul. The soul bears the characteristics of the spirit and the body. The spirit is the motivating force behind the soul, while the body is the means to express the soul.

To put it all together, man is a tripartite being, composed of body, soul, and spirit. As such, in that state, he is created completely; he has everything he needs. *"By his divine power, God has given us everything we need for living a godly life. We have received all of this by coming to know him, the one who called us to himself by means of his marvelous glory and excellence." (2 Peter 1:3).*

---

5   Watchman Nee, *The Spiritual Man,* (California, Living Stream Ministry, 1998)

Through his spirit, man communicates with the spiritual world or the internal realm of the spirit, which is connected to his Creator. Through his body and his five senses, man connects with and communicates with the external environment, and with his divine given will, he can choose to obey the dictates of the external environment, or he can choose to obey the dictates of his internal environment, his spirit, which is directly linked to the Holy Spirit of God. If he decides to obey the dictates of the external environment, he will not experience abundance, but if he chooses to obey the dictates of the Holy Spirit, he will experience abundance, fulfillment, joy, and peace.

I went into that in-depth explanation of the soul, intuition, and spirit of man before introducing you to the Divine Coach, the person here to help you navigate life more efficiently and without stress. This should bring you a sense of relief to know that you don't have to rely on your human wisdom, knowledge, and understanding to navigate through your life. I intended to give you a clearer understanding of the Divine Coach as we go into the next section, which is key to this book.

The Divine Coach – Who He Isn't

Before I explain to you who the Divine Coach is, I will first discuss who He is *not*. You already read that the Divine Coach should not be mistaken for your sixth sense, your conscience, or the voice of your intuition. He is also not a dove, fire, water, wind, or any other symbols that He is often referred to in the scriptures. To be clear, He may manifest His divine power and nature using physical bodies like doves and natural elements to communicate with us, but He is not any of these things. He is a person.

The Divine Coach: Who He Is

I grew up as a Roman Catholic Christian, and at that time, I was taught that the Trinity, God the Father, God the Son, and God the Holy Spirit were one person; that concept I never understood. The best I could make of that concept was that God was one person, but He had different personalities, performing three different functions depending on the need and the environment. I guess I was confused like Phillip the Apostle when he asked Jesus to show him the Father, and Jesus answered:

> *"Don't you know me, Philip, even after I have been among you for such a long time? Anyone who has seen me has seen the Father. How can you say, 'Show us the Father'? Don't you believe that I am in the Father, and that the Father is in me? The words I say to you I do not speak on my own authority. Rather, it is the Father, living in me, who is doing his work. Believe me when I say that I am in the Father and the Father is in me; or at least believe in the evidence of the works themselves."*
>
> *(John 14:9-11 NIV)*

I did not know about the Holy Spirit. I didn't know who He was and what His role was in the life of believers. I guess you could say that I was as ignorant as the early believers in Ephesus who, when asked if they had received the Holy Spirit when they received Christ, they confessed that they did not know that there was a Holy Spirit, let alone received Him.

I did not know that the Holy Spirit was my Divine Intercessor, Helper, Teacher, Guide, Revealer, Comforter, and Baptiser with power from on high. And, most important of all, I did not realize that the Holy Spirit was also my Divine Counselor. As a Leadership Coach by profession, I also need a coach to coach me and hold me accountable for the goals I set for myself. But, what happens when I need more than human counsel, because human counsel is limited and is prone to fail? When human counsel fails, this is when I need divine counsel and guidance.

Up to that time in my life, my main prayer was directed to God the Father, and during those times, prayer was very difficult. I did not know how to pray and that I had a helper who could help me pray and intercede on my behalf. My main prayer was rote and prepared for me by the spiritual authority figures in my life. I was told that I need to ask departed souls who were now called Saints, those who had lived a godly life while they were here on earth, according to the Catholic Church leadership, to help take my requests to God. So, I directed those prepared written prayers to my Patron Saint, Blessed Martin de Porres, so he could take my requests to the Father for me. At times, I would pray to Mary, the Mother of Jesus, for help according to the teachings I received. Being the mother of Jesus, Mary knew Him better than I did, so she would be better able to convince Jesus to help me, but I wanted to communicate with my father in my own words and hear His voice responding to me. However, I was not entirely sure how I could speak to God or know that it was His voice I heard. I also wanted to develop a relationship with Him to share with Him the things that were on my heart, and that mattered to me. I wanted not only to speak my heart to Him, but I wanted to hear His voice as I did at age nine consistently. I did not realize that I needed a real-life challenge that would take me to that place.

At 13 years old, I was studying for the General Certificate of Education, Ordinary Level Examination. This was the exam that I needed to pass in order to graduate from Secondary school and be able to apply for a well-paying job either with the government or with one of the commercial banks. I also needed to continue educating myself so that I could negotiate at an even higher level in society. This was my goal, and this was the trajectory I was on to have a good life. So, I proceeded to ask my spiritual leaders at the church I attended for help, and this was when I was advised to pray to Blessed Martin de Porres for help. The prayer was specific, and he was to ask God the Father to help me pass that exam. I was a diligent student, so I studied hard, prayed hard, and sat the exam when it was time.

It was difficult, but I trusted that with Blessed Martin's help, I would be successful.

Unfortunately, I did not pass all the subjects I needed to be able to graduate and get that well-paying job. I needed at least three but succeeded in passing only one, and guess which one, Biblical Knowledge. I was very disappointed, and I thought long and hard about what could have gone wrong. The only answer I could come up with is that Blessed Martin did not take my prayer to God. So, guess what? I decided that I would not depend on him any longer. I could not trust him to represent my request to God or even represent it well. I decided that I would take my request to my Father myself. After all, my grandmother had told me that God is my Father, and whatsoever I wanted, I could ask Him for it, and He will grant me the desires of my heart. So this is exactly what I did. I prayed every day to God in my language. I asked Him for help and the ability to understand the material I was studying and to help me commit them to memory. The day I went to re-sit the exam, I prayed sincerely to God to be with me while I was writing and to help me remember all I had studied. I trusted that He was listening to me. In fact, I felt assured that He was hearing me and that He would help me, and this time, when the results came back, I had succeeded in passing four subjects. I was then 15 years of age, and I needed these subjects to convince employers that at the tender age of 15, I was capable of holding a job. I was convinced then that God had heard my prayer, and I didn't need to have a Saint as a mediator; I could call on God myself.

About six months later, a missionary came to our home and confirmed that I was right. He introduced me to a new life in Christ Jesus. With his guidance, I prayed a simple prayer, a prayer of repentance, and I committed to living my life based on the principles of the Bible and immediately felt the need to know God better. So, I started reading, studying, and meditating in the Holy Scriptures and continued praying daily to God for help in developing an intimate relationship with Jesus Christ.

Encountering The Divine Coach

One day, while reading the Holy Scriptures, I encountered the person of the Holy Spirit in the book of John chapter 14. In that chapter, Jesus, knowing that He was soon to depart from the world, was leaving the disciples alone. The time had come for them to be introduced to the Holy Spirit, their Helper, Teacher, Guide, and Counselor. Jesus said, *"If you love me, keep my commands. And I will ask the Father, and he will give you another advocate to help you and be with you forever, the Spirit of truth. The world cannot accept him, because it neither sees him nor knows him. But you know him, for he lives with you and will be in you....All this I have spoken while still with you. But the Advocate, the Holy Spirit, whom the Father will send in my name, will teach you all things and will remind you of everything I have said to you"* (John 14:15, 25-26 NIV).

As I grew older and continued to stay in the scriptures, I began to do an intentional study on who the Holy Spirit was, what His functions were in the life of believers, and how we could effectively partner with Him to have the abundant life Christ came to give us. As I continued on that path of inquiry and learned more of the Holy Spirit, I decided that it was appropriate to call Him my Divine Coach. In fact, He has become even more than a coach to me in my profession as a Human Development Specialist, specializing in the area of organizational leadership development, leadership coaching, and mentoring, specifically to faith-based leaders. He has been operating in my life, performing all the functions Jesus identified He would perform in the lives of the early disciples and apostles. So, for the purpose of this book, I refer to the Holy Spirit as the Divine Coach, even though at times I often use the two names interchangeably.

Who He Is

The Holy Spirit is the third person of the Godhead whose major role is to communicate messages to us from our Father in Heaven. God speaks his many messages to us through His Holy Spirit, but His messages are not always easy to understand, pleasant to human ears, or obeyed. Just as a professional life or business coach does not always tell his/her clients what they want to hear, the Divine Coach, our master coach, does not always tell us what we love to hear. Receiving awesome prophetic words or words of knowledge from Him that bring immediate results is nice, but at times, the Divine Coach, God's voice, will lead you and test you like He tested Abraham. He asked Abraham to give up His only son, whom he loved, and He may ask you to give up something you are attached to. When and if He does, be encouraged that inherent in that test is the grace to do what He is asking you to do, and an even greater blessing is attached to it. Philippians 2:13 states, "For it is God which worketh in you both to will and to do of his good pleasure." God works with us and in us through His Holy Spirit, empowering us to do all that He called us to do and to be all He called us to be. That is the definition of grace, God's empowering presence within you and me to accomplish His divine will.

To receive that grace, we must be obedient to that empowering presence of the third person of the Godhead. Many believers desire to receive that empowering presence. They want God to work in their lives with signs and wonders as he worked in the disciples' lives, but they want to receive power without obedience. Obedience is the price we must pay for the anointing of God. To see the level of anointing in operation in our lives as the early believers experienced, we must pay that price. The price of the anointing is obedience. God wants our lives to be totally devoted to Him. He is not asking us to sacrifice material things. He is asking for our entire devotion and dedication.

If you want to go deeper in God and with God, you must obey the Holy Spirit's leading. If you disobey, you will stay on the same level. You will not grow into all that God has called you to be and do. By obeying the promptings of the Holy Spirit, your Divine Coach, you allow Him to develop within you the fruit of His character. This is the fruit of love, joy, peace, patience, goodness, gentleness, kindness, faith, and self-control mentioned in Galatians 5:21-23. As you obey His voice and you submit to Him, He, in turn, will develop His fruit within you. His fruit is His attitude toward you. This fruit can't be developed if you are disobedient to Him or if you grieve Him. Fortunately, God will help you in your desire to be obedient. You do not have to do it alone.

CHAPTER V

The Role of the Divine Coach in the Life of The Believer

"I will not leave you as orphans [comfortless, bereaved, and helpless]; I will come [back] to you."

John 14:18 AMP

It's comforting to know that as believers, we do not have to live our lives alone. Our Divine Coach intervenes in our lives to provide us with supernatural power, wisdom, revelation, and direction. As previously discussed, the Divine Coach is your helper. He will not intervene when you are able to act on your behalf. He will only intervene when your natural human strength fails and you need His divine intervention, guidance, protection, and healing. The Divine Coach's intervention sometimes comes in the form of divine revelations, dreams, and visions. At other times, He speaks directly to our spirits; still, at other times, He ministers to us by giving us divine messages from the Word of God, through Pastors and the spiritual communication gifts in the body of Christ such as prophecy, words of knowledge, and words of wisdom.

Supernatural Intervention

One of the many ways the Divine Coach works is to heal our bodies supernaturally. I have been privileged to experience several supernatural healings. On Thanksgiving Eve several years ago. I was in the kitchen preparing dinner for friends and family members that were expected to arrive the next day. I wanted to have most of the dinner prepared so I could dedicate my time to interacting with my guests, so the dinner preparation took most of the night into early the next morning. At about 2:00 am in the morning, I began feeling some painful discomfort in my lower back after standing and cooking for most of the night. I decided to lie on my couch in the living room and wait for the turkey to be finished so I could go to bed. After about an hour, I rose from the couch to go and check on the turkey, and I felt a sharp pain from the lower part of my back on the right side, which radiated all the way down my right leg to my heel. The pain was so excruciating that I could not move. Apart from the pain of giving birth to my son, I had never felt anything as painful as that in any part of my body before. After a few minutes, I managed to pull myself up from the couch painfully, and I literally dragged myself into the kitchen to remove the turkey from the oven.

The pain continued after that day and grew progressively worse despite several months of physical therapy. At times it was so difficult to get around that I had to be driven to my physical therapy sessions. I managed to get some modicum of relief from the physical therapy sessions but not enough to function effectively. Eventually, I had to submit to receiving cortisone shots and epidural injections in my upper and lower back.

As a woman of faith, I continued to pray for God's healing intervention during those months while receiving physical therapy, epidural injections, and cortisone shots. Around that same time, my son's dad, who lived in the Islands, died. I decided to accompany my son to the funeral since he had not lived on the island because he had left home when he was quite young. We purchased our ticket and our flight was scheduled to leave at 7:30am that day. Since he lived closer to Regan National Airport, the plan was that

I would meet him at home and we would drive to the airport together. The day came for us to leave. I got up at 4:30am to get ready. I tried to turn over on my right side to put my right leg onto the floor, but I couldn't move. That same excruciating pain that I had experienced on that Thanksgiving Eve gripped me again. It was so painful that I cried out to God. I said a prayer of faith which I will never forget to this day. I prayed:

> *"Lord, if You have finished using me…If you no longer want me to travel to Africa to visit the orphans and vulnerable youths I have committed myself to empower through education…If that commitment was my decision and You had nothing to do with it…If You are through with me ministering to Your people, that's okay."*

> *"I will cancel my trip and remain here. I will see this as Your way of saying it's time to retire. But, Lord, if it is Your will to continue to use me, I ask You to please heal me now so that I can go on my trip. In that way, I will know that You are not done with me yet. I will continue working on expanding Your Kingdom and bringing glory to Your name."*

As I finished praying these words, I heard that familiar voice of the Holy Spirit say to me, "Get up. Go and take your shower." I stood up without question. The Holy Spirit, my Divine Healer, had healed my body. The pain was gone, and it has never returned to this day. I had experienced the miraculous healing power of the Holy Spirit.

Natural Intervention

In addition to manifesting His supernatural healing power in our lives, the Divine Coach works by using all the natural gifts He has gifted us. He uses advancement in medical science, technology, biology, engineering, education, arts and entertainment, space exploration, and travel, to name a few. In this way, God uses man's natural giftings to manifest Himself in the earth. When we become born again and filled with the Holy Spirit, our Divine Coach distributes supernatural gifts to us and partners with us by providing for us, healing us, delivering us, teaching us, counseling us, and consoling us so that we can enjoy the abundant life Jesus came to give us. In that way, God is glorified in the Body of Christ, and God's Kingdom is expanded in the earth.

You, too, can experience the divine intervention of the Holy Spirit in your life if only you will reach out to Him. Also, when human intervention is not available, He will respond swiftly with His supernatural intervention. He will not only heal you, but He will also intervene and empower you to continue to fulfill God's divine plan in your life. For according to Jeremiah 29:11, *"God has a plan for you , a plan to bless you and not to harm you. To give you hope and a future"* and to take you all the way to the expected end He has for you, and that is the main reason why you need the Divine Coach in your life.

Why does He Intervene?

The Divine Coach is your Divine Deliverer. He intervenes in your life for various reasons, one of which is to deliver you from evil. Scripture affirms that when the enemy comes in like a flood, the Holy Spirit will lift up a standard inside of you and me to deliver us. He will always manifest His presence… for divine deliverance.

The Bible recorded many instances when the Devil presented himself in the lives of God's people to kill, steal, or destroy them, and the Divine Coach had to intervene. He tried to destroy the three Hebrew boys, Shadrach Meshach and Abednego, on one such occasion. Upon the advice of the enemies of these three young men, the King of Babylon agreed to kill them for not worshiping him by throwing them into a furnace of fire. God had to send an angel who miraculously saved them from the flames

LIVE YOUR LIFE FROM THE INSIDE OUT

of the fire. On another occasion, God literally delivered Daniel out of a den of lions for a similar reason by sending an angel to prevent the lions from killing Daniel. God does not only use supernatural means to deliver us – He also uses natural means. When Hayman, an enemy of the Jews, wanted to annihilate the entire Jewish race in Sussa, through a series of natural strategies revealed to Queen Esther, God delivered the Jews out of the hands of their enemy Hayman. The Holy Spirit intervenes to deliver us from the hands of the enemy. He is our deliverer.

What Are The Outcomes of His Intervention?

The first thing that the Divine Coach wants to do if you allow Him is to bring power into your life. Power to do and be more than you can imagine! Before Jesus went back to Heaven, He cautioned His disciples one last time not to attempt to fulfill their divine calling without the help of the Holy Spirit. He explained to them that they needed His divine intervention to receive the power which was absolutely necessary for them to be effective. A careful study of the book of Acts reveals God through His Spirit working miracles in human lives. In Acts 1:8 (NLT), Jesus assures them in this way, "But you will receive power when the Holy Spirit comes upon you. And you will be my witnesses, telling people about me everywhere in Jerusalem, throughout Judea, in Samaria, and to the ends of the earth."

Jesus assured them of the transforming power of the Holy Spirit. For instance, He transformed the life of Paul, a religious leader steeped in Jewish Old Testament thought, so dramatically that He dedicated the rest of his life to spreading the good news of the gospel of Jesus Christ. He transformed the life of Lydia, a prosperous Jewish businesswoman, the Philippian jailer, and a middle-class Roman civil servant. The divine power of the Holy Spirit changed the lives of these once ordinary men and women, empowering them to do extraordinary things for God. This would never have happened without the intervention of the Divine Coach.

The second outcome of the intervention of the Divine Coach in the life of a believer is the impartation of spiritual gifts. The gifts of the Spirit are laid out in 1 Corinthians 12:8-11 and speak to things such as miraculous healing, wisdom, prophecy, speaking in tongues, and discernment. These gifts were manifested 2,000 years ago, but they are still alive and well in our own lives today! Through personal experience and the testimonies of others, I have seen these gifts in action in places like Africa, Latin America, and the Caribbean. Every time they have shown themselves, they have blessed the individual recipient of the gift and glorified God in the process.

The Holy Spirit meets people where they are, but He does not leave them there. In His presence, they are changed, and their lives are transformed. The Holy Spirit still reaches people in all spectrums of society. His power to transform reaches both men and women, rich and poor, educated and uneducated. You can see the Holy Spirit's power breaking through cultural barriers and belief systems, triumphing over cultural biases, transforming lifelong, deeply ingrained habits, and teaching all of humanity Christ's grace and truth.

The Divine Coach is the Holy Spirit of God. He is the perfect gift of God to all those who believe in and love Jesus Christ as their Lord, Savior, Redeemer, and Master. The Holy Spirit is an eternal spirit that lives in time. He lives in us and with us, and no matter how we describe that voice, we know that He is the voice of power, wisdom, revelation, knowledge, and understanding. In other words, He speaks within us to reveal things to us that we would not otherwise know through our natural senses. To the unbeliever, He is the voice of intuition, sixth sense, conscience, reason, and inner voice. The Divine Coach indwells the believer. To the believer, He is the gift of God to us to help us live our lives from the inside out. Under the guidance and direction of the Divine Coach, we access that unlimited divine power that is within us.

CHAPTER VI

Hearing The Voice of The Divine Coach

"My sheep hear my voice, and I know them, and they follow me. I give them eternal life, and they will never perish, and no one will snatch them out of my hand."

John 10:27 KJV

We hear the voice of the Divine Coach in myriads of ways. He speaks to us in dreams and visions in the night. I remember dreaming about the events of 911 on the night of August 28th, 2001. I had no clue what was going to happen. I remember vividly that I was in this tall building, and as I looked across the room, another building of equal height crumbled before my very eyes. Before I had time to make sense of what I saw, the building in which I was located started to shake vehemently under my feet. At that moment, a huge hand just miraculously lifted the floor I was on and placed it safely on the ground, and I stepped safely out of a broken window. Then, I looked and saw dead bodies all around me. Sirens were blaring, and people were running in all directions shouting, "get out of the city, get out of the city." I started running and running until I came to a safe place where I could stop and rest. I remembered thinking it was not safe for me to rest until I could get to my son and his family to let them know that they should avoid going into the city. I woke up from the dream tired and confused, but I knew that the Divine Coach was communicating an important life event to come, except at the time, I did not know what that life event was. This was not the first time I had been warned of tsunamis, floods, and political unrest around the world.

I called my husband immediately and shared the dream with him, and asked him to pray. I also shared the dream with one of my prayer partners and asked her to join me in praying for the country and our families. We asked for the intervention of the Divine Coach to spare our nation from disaster and to spare our families from harm and danger.

I know now that the Holy Spirit was revealing to me in that dream not only of the events that took place on 911, but specifically, He was warning me of impending danger in my life as well. The significance of the dream is that I was saved from taking the flight that left Dulles that went down over Pennsylvania. My late husband and I were scheduled to take that flight to go to a conference in California that day. Fortunately, he was away on an international business trip and got delayed; that delay saved our lives.

Interestingly, I am writing this part of the book on the 20th anniversary of the events of 911. Had it not been for the intimate relationship I developed over the years with the Divine Coach and my ability to hear His voice speaking to me from within and more importantly, had it not been for my ability to tune out the external environment of the world, I would not have heard the voice of the Divine Coach in that dream.

Life challenges and life events can cause us not to recognize the voice of the Holy Spirit, our Divine Coach. As a result, instead of being guided by His inner wisdom, we may rely on our own understanding of things. Sometimes we tend to rely on our education, knowledge, past experiences, thoughts, feelings, and human reasoning. When we can no longer lean on our own understanding, we seek the counsel of others.

It is not natural for us to seek the inner voice of wisdom that we have been endowed with to help us respond to life challenges. When our reaction is to rely on ourselves or others, we ignore the voice of the Divine Coach. Effectively we drown out or quench His voice. In 1 Thessalonians 5:19, the Bible admonishes us to be careful not to quench the Holy Spirit with which we were sealed unto the day of salvation.

Our dominant culture makes it so easy to quench or oppose the Divine Coach's work in our lives by walking in pride and stubbornness, which directly opposes the Holy Spirit. When I reflect on the language we use to talk about our life challenges, it is evident that most of us, including myself, tend to lean on our understanding rather than trust God. Instead of humbling ourselves in prayer and seeking God when faced with life challenges, the common response is to seek the counsel of others or to worry.

We must be willing to humbly invite God into our life's challenges rather than conforming to solve them in the ways of the world. Only then can we truly be salt and light as Christ calls us to be in this dark world. Christians in our society today are getting divorced, suffering from depression, being addicted to over-the-counter drugs, and suffering from obesity, just like the people in the world. This tells me that instead of trusting in God, we address our problems just like the world. Instead of being salt and light, we are contributing to the darkness in the world. In doing so, we are impeding the work of the Holy Spirit. Those who desire to follow our Lord Jesus Christ must be willing to submit themselves to God and resist the sensationalism promoted by the dominant culture. We must be willing to clothe ourselves with humility in dealing with one another and responding to life challenges.

Recognizing His Voice

The Divine Coach is always speaking, but to recognize his voice, we must first know how He communicates to us. Let me ask you this question, why do we speak? Well, allow me to answer this – we speak for a variety of reasons. One of the main reasons we speak is to communicate our intentions and emotions in a language that can be understood. All human relationships are formed, sustained, and terminated through our speech.

Just as we have specific reasons why we communicate with each other, so, too, God has reasons why He communicates with us, and, being created in the image and likeness of God, He communicates in much the same way as we do. He communicates His intentions and His emotions; He is always speaking, but we may not always recognize His voice or understand His intentions. To recognize God's voice from among all the other voices in the environment, we must first establish a relationship with Him and seek to develop that relationship with the help of the Holy Spirit.

So, why does God speak to us? When God speaks His intent is to help us create the life we want and to help us bring every part of our lives into divine order. Divine order is extremely important to God. We know that because it was the first thing He did when He created the world. In the creation account in Genesis 1:3-31, the scriptures tell us that the world was without form and void, and there was darkness all around. God, in partnership with the Holy Spirit, stepped into that void and filled it. He called for light, and the Holy Spirit created light. Effectively we see the Holy Spirit in partnership with God the Father carrying out every word of God's command. God speaks to bring order out of chaos, fill up voids, and bring light where there is darkness in our lives.

God also speaks when He wants to guide, protect, heal and empower us. He does so with one goal in mind, to expand His Kingdom here on the earth as it is in Heaven. God's ultimate goal is for us to live an abundant, fulfilled life here on this earth, but in order for us to experience all of these fantastic benefits, we must first establish an effective partnership with the Holy Spirit. This partnership is established through obedience. Just as God partnered with the Holy Spirit to fulfill all His desires when He created the world, so too must we create an effective partnership with the Holy Spirit to experience that life of abundance, but, first, we must be able to hear and recognize the voice of the Holy Spirit. Hearing and recognizing the Holy Spirit's voice is the only way to establish that divine partnership so that we experience abundant life.

Hearing His Voice

Countless people have asked this question throughout the ages, *"How can I be sure that I am hearing the voice of God?"* If you are like most Christians, you too must have wondered how you can differentiate your voice and the voice of God from among the many voices around you. How can you, for example, differentiate between your voice, that is, the voice of your emotions, the voice of your flesh, and the voice of your greatest enemy, Satan himself?

As simple as it is to call on God, sometimes we have a hard time distinguishing between God's voice, the voice of the external environment, our selfish desires, and the voice of our enemy, Satan or the Devil as he is called. If we want to have a solid relationship with God and walk boldly as believers, we must know which voice speaks to us. Is it God's voice you are hearing, or is it Satan's voice? If it is Satan's voice you are hearing, you will want to know because obeying his voice leads to, among other things, panic, fear, illness, death, and destruction. Here are five ways to distinguish between God's voice and Satan's voice.

God's Voice Doesn't Cause Panic. It Calms You.

One of the surest ways to distinguish between God's voice and Satan's voice is to ask yourself if what you hear causes you to feel a sense of panic or peace. Satan uses our emotions to deceive us. Usually, when it's Satan's voice, you will be left feeling incredibly anxious. It won't feel like there is any peace in your heart. We know from Scripture that our God is a God of peace.

One of the names of God is Jehovah Shalom – Shalom means Peace. Jesus is known as the Prince of Peace. 2 Thessalonians 3:16 says, "Now may the LORD of peace Himself give you peace at all times in every way…" and Psalm 29:11 says, "The LORD gives strength to His people, the LORD blesses His people with peace." If you feel like your inner sense of peace is lost, it may be the devil at work, not the Holy Spirit. That voice of peace distinguishes among the voices of the world, the voice of Satan, and the voice of our selfish desires. All of these external voices have one distinguishing characteristic, commotion.

God's voice doesn't feel like commotion. As believers, we must be aware that our enemy Satan will use anything He can to cause commotion in our lives. We must be careful not to listen to any voice that is feeling like or even causing anything like commotion in our spirit. This is why it's imperative that we turn down the commotion occurring in our lives so we can clearly hear God's voice. Sometimes, it will feel like God is silent, but the truth is He is always present. Jeremiah 33:3 says, "Call to Me, and I will answer you and will tell you great and hidden things that you have not known." If you feel like there is a great deal of chaos going on in your life, this may simply be Satan stirring up trouble. You must tune out the enemy's commotion so you can draw closer to God.

God's Voice Confirms His Word. It Doesn't Contradict

A tell-tale sign that you're listening to Satan's voice and not God's voice is if it contradicts God's Word. Satan will tell you that it's okay to sin and that the sin you're committing won't damage the people around you. This couldn't be further from the truth. We are called to obey God's commandments. Deuteronomy 5:33 says, "Walk in obedience to all that the LORD your God has commanded you, so that you may live and prosper and prolong your days in the land that you will possess." If the voice you're hearing is leading you to sin and go against God's Word, it isn't of God.

God's Voice Strengthens Your Prayer Life

The world as we know it today is filled with commotion and chaos. There are so many things that are vying for our time and attention. In our relationship with God, as Christians, we are called to pray without ceasing (1 Thessalonians 5:17). In fact, it is advisable that we set aside time to pray daily. Philippians 4:6 says, "Do not be anxious about anything, but in everything by prayer and supplication with thanksgiving, let your requests be made known to God."

Satan will spend time trying to pull you away from your time with God. The voice of the world, that is, your busy schedule, will not encourage you to pray because that voice tells you that you have too many other important things going on. If you're having trouble praying, then you should be aware that maybe it is the voice of your aspirations and your schedule speaking to you and discouraging you from praying.

Some may say that they are hearing the devil's voice but beware that you do not blame the devil for everything going on in your life. You have the ability to take action when you want to see changes in your life. So when you are distracted because of your busy schedule, the way to counteract this is first to call on God and ask Him to open your heart again to active prayer. James 4:8 says, "Draw near to God, and He will draw near to you." Then, be intentional and schedule time in your calendar to pray. Then go a step further and make the sacrifice to honor that calendar entry daily. Be sure to set that time up to succeed. If you are an early morning person, pray in the morning. If you are a night person, schedule time at night.

God wants you to be close to Him each day, and prayer is the best opportunity to draw near to Him. God has given us the Holy Spirit to help us pray when we do not know what or how to pray. Allow Him to help you by simply asking Him to. You will be surprised by the response you will receive. It won't be long before you have found a prayer partner in the person of the Holy Spirit.

Prayer, fasting, and reading the word of God are three great tools to help you hear the voice of God. We will return to these tools and strategies and discuss them later on in the book. For now, I encourage you to set aside time in your busy schedule for those three spiritual practices. In this way, you will hide the Word in your heart such that when life challenges come your way, you can access the word you stored within so that you can make wise and informed choices and decisions instead of leaning on your own understanding.

God's Voice Uplifts You. It Doesn't Make You Feel Worthless

The voice of God is uplifting. It never condemns you or makes you feel worthless. Jesus assures us that He didn't come into the world to condemn the world. "For God did not send his Son into the world to condemn the world, but to save the world through him (John 3:17). He came to save the world from the destructive intent of Satan. "To this end was the Son of God manifested, that he might destroy the works of the Devil" (1 John 2:8). One of Satan's greatest tricks is to convince you that you are worthless. Over time, you begin to become convinced that you are no longer valuable to God or anyone else. You begin to ask yourself things like, "If God loved me, why am I experiencing this?" This is Satan planting seeds of doubt in your head so that you will disconnect from God; know that this is not of God. Satan wants nothing more for you but to doubt God and the value of your life. If he can trick you into thinking this, he can move you far away from God. God wants the opposite, He wants to uplift you, and He wants you to know how important you are. You are not worthless, you are important to God. Believe the word of God about you. He loved you so much that He gave His life for you. He restored you to your original position in Him so that you can go out and add value to those you are called to. You are not useless – you are valuable and capable of bringing tremendous value to this planet.

Right now, it's time to pause and listen to what voices are speaking to you. If something is going on in your life that is blocking you from hearing God's voice, you must take courageous action and remove it from your space. If, for example, you identify a situation in your life that is undermining one of the fruits of the Spirit from manifesting itself in you or anything that will harm you or harm another person, then it is your responsibility to take intentional action to get rid of that situation.

Acknowledge it, confess it, ask God for help and do your part to get rid of it. This is what the Bible refers to as sin. Psalm 66:18 says, "If I had not confessed the sin in my heart, the LORD would not have listened." Call on God this very moment and restore your relationship with Him.

The voice of God is only distinguished and heard by those who are in a relationship with Him through Jesus Christ. We hear His voice in His Word and when we are speaking to Him in prayer. We also hear His voice more clearly when we are fasting and meditating on His Word. God's children never mistake His voice for another because His voice encourages, heals, and brings peace. The more time you spend speaking with God, the easier it is to distinguish His voice and be able to incorporate His voice in your life.

CHAPTER VII

The Holy Spirit: Our Helper

"The Holy Spirit illuminates the minds of people, makes us yearn for God, and takes spiritual truth and makes it understandable to us."

–Billy Graham

When I think of the Holy Spirit, I primarily think of Him as God with us, helping and empowering us to live a flourishing life that radiates the goodness of God. The Holy Spirit is a beautiful and powerful part of who God is and who you are. However, you need Him in your life as a conduit to become who God created you to be. Through His divine power, we can have His aid in all situations. Without Him, we are powerless. Paul understood this so well that in 2 Thessalonians 1:11, he told the believers, "With this in mind, we constantly pray for you, that our God may make you worthy of his calling, and that by his power He may bring to fruition your every desire for goodness and your every deed prompted by faith."

I don't know about you, but I'm constantly aware of my need for divine help. As my flesh fights for control, it's the Spirit that steps in and helps me to be who God created me to be. The Holy Spirit is our Helper, and it is the one function every believer must confidently seek. Jesus assured us of that in John 16:7, *"Nevertheless, I tell you the truth: it is to your advantage that I go away, for if I do not go away, the Helper will not come to you. But if I go, I will send him to you."* However, in order to receive His help, we must ask for it.

Accessing the help of the Holy Spirit is critical to experience the abundant life Christ came to ensure we have. In order to gain access to His help, you must have a relationship with Him, and there are several ways you can develop a relationship with Him. One of the ways we ask for His help which most believers are familiar with is through intercessory prayer.

The Holy Spirit Helps Us To Pray

The Holy Spirit is your Divine Intercessor, and He intercedes on your behalf at all times. He represents our needs to God the Father when we pray in the name of Jesus. When you need His help, no matter what the need is, He is sent to help us. You can rest assured that He hears you when you pray and ask for His help. According to John 5:14-15, He will answer you when you ask for help as long as your requests align to the will of God. *"And this is the confidence that we have toward him, that if we ask anything according to his will he hears us. And if we know that he hears us in whatever we ask, we know that we have the requests that we have asked of him."* Therefore, whenever you have a need, you can confidently reach out to Him in prayer. He will represent your need to God, who is always willing and capable of meeting your need.

The Holy Spirit Helps You When You Are Weak

As your Father, God is your provider, and He wants to meet your every need; however, you must be humble enough to ask. Don't allow pride and fear to keep you from asking for His help. God wants us to ask the Holy

Spirit for His help. The Holy Spirit was sent to strengthen you when you are weak. As you strive to live your life from the inside out, you won't always feel courageous and strong. When you feel powerless, tired, or like you're failing at life, you can have confidence as a believer that you're not alone.

> *"Have I not commanded you? Be strong and courageous. Do not be afraid; do not be discouraged, for the LORD your God will be with you wherever you go."*
>
> *(Joshua 1:9)*

How wonderful it must feel when someone can come alongside us and bear our burdens as we step aside and get some rest. The Holy Spirit is there to fight our battles. We can start each day knowing the Holy Spirit is there to help us. He is the power that sustains, energizes, and keeps us on a holy path. Do not hesitate to call on Him for help and invite Him into all of your life situations. You will find that life will become more joyful and fulfilling when you invite Him to partner with you.

The Holy Spirit is Your Divine Teacher

> *"But the Advocate, the Holy Spirit, whom the Father will send in my name, will teach you all things and will remind you of everything I have said to you."*
>
> *(John 14:26)*

While Jesus was on earth, He was called Rabbi. A Rabbi in the Jewish religion was a qualified teacher of the Torah or the Holy Scriptures, but Jesus was no ordinary teacher. According to Matthew 7:29, "He taught them with authority, and not like their scribes." A Rabbi usually had disciples or followers, and that is why when Jesus began His public ministry, He chose men to become His disciples. Having been with Jesus for three years, it is understandable that His disciples would depend on His teachings. One of Jesus' major functions was to train His disciples and prepare them for public ministry. Obviously, Jesus had to provide His followers with another teacher equally capable and powerful to carry on where He left off. Teaching is one of the roles of the Holy Spirit.

The Holy Spirit is Our Divine Revealer

The Holy Spirit is also our Divine Revealer. As our Divine Revealer, He teaches us all things, reveals spiritual truths, and gives us insight into the word of God not evident to the human eye. The whole objective of God sending the Holy Spirit is to teach us to open our minds to understand spiritual things that are confusing. Today, the Holy Spirit, our teacher, helps us to have an amazing understanding of the mind of Christ and the will of God for us. Have you ever had one of those moments when you were in a situation and a Scripture verse you read or memorized years ago popped into your head, encouraging you at that moment? That was the Holy Spirit reminding you of what you had been taught. He will always help you to recall what you've read in Scripture. He empowers you with understanding and the ability to recall important verses that apply to your life.

This knowledge and understanding of the Holy Spirit are critical to believers to expand the Kingdom, especially in these days when Christ is not known and so grossly misunderstood. Now, more than ever, when there are so many false teachers in the world claiming to know the Holy Spirit, we need the teaching and the revelation of the Holy Spirit to live an empowered life. However, the Holy Spirit only works with those who have received Jesus Christ as personal Lord and Savior and who are prepared to obey His divine guidance and direction.

Obedience Brings His Help

Although the Holy Spirit has been sent to help believers, 1 Corinthians 2:20 confirms that there are conditions to receiving the help of the Divine Coach. One of those conditions is love for Jesus. Jesus confirms in John 14:23, "Anyone who loves me will obey my teaching." The other condition which is inextricably related and is equally important is obedience. "Anyone who doesn't love me will not obey my teaching" (John 14:26). The Apostle Peter confirms in Acts 5:32 that the Holy Spirit is only "given to those who obey Him." Jesus obeyed the Holy Spirit, and therefore He operated in the powerful anointing of the Holy Spirit.

In Jesus, we find the perfect model of obedience. As His disciples, we should follow His example as well as His commands. Over and over again, we read in the Bible that God blesses and rewards obedience. Genesis 22:18 states, "And through your descendants, all the nations of the earth will be blessed all because you have obeyed me." Luke 11:28 records, "Jesus replied, 'But even more blessed are all who hear the word of God and put it into practice.'"

Obedience calls for intentional action. Don't just listen to God's word, you have to be a doer; otherwise, you will only be fooling yourself. For if you listen to the word and don't obey, it is like glancing at your face in a mirror. You see yourself, walk away, and forget what you look like, but if you look carefully into the perfect law that sets you free, and if you do what it says and don't forget what you heard, then God will bless you for doing it (James 1:22–25 NLT). If you want to receive the help of the Holy Spirit, you must be obedient to Him. There are several benefits to obedience to the Holy Spirit; I discuss these benefits later in the book.

The Divine Coach Sanctifies Us For Works of Righteousness

As our helper, the Divine Coach helps us in the process of sanctification. This is the process every believer must go through to become more like

Christ. To be "sanctified" means to be set apart as sacred. Essentially, it's the purification of sin and spiritually maturing to become more Christlike. In 1 Corinthians 6:11, Paul confirms our position in Christ through the work of the Divine Coach. Here is what he says: *"But you were washed, you were sanctified, you were justified in the name of the Lord Jesus Christ and by the Spirit of our God."*

Sanctification is an all-important process for a believer. Through this process, with the help of the Divine Coach, the believer can leave behind old habits and become a new person by adapting new behaviors and habits. Only by the power of the Divine Coach can old bad habits be broken and be replaced by good ones. The sanctification process is not instant; it usually happens gradually over time. As a believer faces life's challenges and adversities, the Divine Coach aids in this maturation process, thus setting him/her apart as they mature for good works.

The Divine Coach wants to help you in this process of sanctification by helping you put away those old bad habits, which the Bible describes as dying to the flesh or your old self. In this process, the believer must be intentional, that is, you are to make every effort in your daily life to be all that God created you to be. You must be free from the entanglement or the bondage of sin so that you can make the intentional choice to obey the voice of the Divine Coach as life challenges come your way. Your obedience will result in you responding to the challenges instead of reacting, thereby living victoriously. Remember, though, that you cannot do this alone. You must allow the Divine Coach to complete that sanctification process within you to make you more like Christ.

The Divine Coach Makes Us More Like Christ

Every believer should desire to be more like Christ. The more we spend time in His word and His presence, the desire becomes greater. However, this desire cannot be realized without the help of the Divine Coach. In 2 Corinthians 3:18, Paul underscores this truth:

"And we all, who with unveiled faces contemplate the Lord's glory, are being transformed into his image with ever-increasing glory, which comes from the Lord, who is the Spirit."

Moses experienced God's glory on the mountaintop, but we have communion with Him every day! When we meditate on God's Word and in it see God's Son, then the Spirit transforms us! We become more like the Lord Jesus Christ as we grow 'from glory to glory." Our goal is Christlikeness, which takes place through the power of the Divine Coach, the Holy Spirit. While we focused on sanctification and the diminishment of sin in the previous point, this is instead a transformation into the image of Christ.

The Divine Coach Empowers Us

The Divine Coach is the empowering presence of God within you, empowering you to do all that God has called you to do and to be all that God has called you to be. He distributes to each believer various spiritual gifts, as Paul explains in 1 Corinthians 12:4-11 NIV:

"There are different kinds of spiritual gifts, but the same Spirit is the source of them all. There are different kinds of service, but we serve the same Lord. God works in different ways, but it is the same God who does the work in all of us. A spiritual gift is given to each of us so we can help each other. To one person the Spirit gives the ability to give wise advice; to another the same Spirit gives a message of special knowledge. The same Spirit gives great faith, to another, and to someone else the one Spirit gives the gift of healing. He gives one person the power to perform miracles, and another the ability to prophesy. He gives someone else the ability to discern whether a message is from the Spirit of God or from another spirit. Still another

person is given the ability to speak in unknown languages, while another is given the ability to interpret what is being said. It is the one and only Spirit who distributes all these gifts. He alone decides which gift each person should have."

* Additional passages of the gifts of the Spirit can be found in Ephesians 4 and Romans 12.

Some of the gifts of the Divine Coach listed in these verses are referred to as power gifts. They are called power gifts because they empower you, the believer, to accomplish extraordinary things for God. Other gifts are leadership gifts and service gifts, often referred to as the fruit of the Spirit. I discuss these fruits in another section of the book. These gifts allow us the grace or the ability to interact with each other and communicate appropriately. In this way, we acknowledge each other and appreciate the contribution we each make in expanding God's Kingdom. The Bible calls this submitting to each other or giving honor to each other

I encourage you to embrace what God has put inside of you and be His instrument for Kingdom purpose! The gift(s) you receive will empower you for the calling God has placed on your life. These empowerment gifts are available to all believers helping them to live a holy life (Acts 2:39). Through the power of the Holy Spirit, we become more like Jesus and are empowered to do the Father's will on this earth, which, primarily, is for us to be bold witnesses to others for Christ (Acts 1:8).

The ultimate objective of the gifts of the Divine Coach is for us to honor God, love each other, and expand the Kingdom together. We accomplish all of this as we yield to the voice and inner workings of the Divine Coach within us. We are encouraged to ask the Holy Spirit to fill us up regularly. When you feel depleted or need strength, ask Him to replenish you (Ephesians 5:18). It's not enough to exist with the belief that the Father and the Son are first and the Holy Spirit is secondary. They are equal and work in harmony with each other.

The uniqueness of the Holy Spirit is His presence within us. Jesus said before He ascended to heaven that the Holy Spirit would come and dwell within us as a believer. He empowers us from within to live victoriously for the cause of Christ and the glory of the Father. The Holy Spirit is a gift to every believer. He was promised by the Father to help us live the abundant life that Christ promised us and our household. That experience of abundance takes place within so that we can live holy lives.

Through Obedience, We Experience the Blessings of Holy Living

When we allow the Divine Coach to transform us from within, we walk in obedience, grow in holiness, and experience the blessings of holy living, which is evidenced by success and prosperity. This is the process of sanctification which can also be described as spiritual growth. The more we read God's Word and allow the Divine Coach to change us from within, the more we grow in obedience and holiness as Christians.

One of the major benefits of obeying the voice of the Divine Coach is success in every area of our lives, including financial prosperity. Such success and prosperity come from spending time meditating on the word of God. In Joshua 1:8, Moses confirms to Joshua that meditating on the word of God and obedience to the word were sure ways to obtaining success and prosperity when they entered the Promised Land. Joshua was about to take over the leadership from Moses to lead the children of Israel into the land flowing with milk and honey, where they were going to experience abundance. Here is what he told Joshua: "This book of the law shall not depart from thy mouth, but you shall meditate upon it day and night and be careful to obey all that is written therein. Then shall you prosper and shall have great success" (Joshua 1:8). When we spend time in the word of God, and we obey the principles therein, we learn to walk in integrity which ultimately leads to prosperity, success, and abundant joy.

These amazing benefits of holy living are the outgrowth of obedience to the word of God. I call them Biblical success principles. The Bible contains many of these success principles, which, when practiced, lead to prosperity, peace, and an abundant life. One of those success principles which I attribute to my financial success is the Biblical principle of Tithing, and I highly recommend it to you. The Biblical principle of Tithing comes from the Old Testament. It is found in the book of Malachi 3:10 (NIV), and it reads:

> *"Bring the whole tithe into the storehouse, so that there may be food in my house. Test me in this," says the Lord Almighty, "and see if I will not throw open the floodgates of heaven and pour out so much blessing that there will not be room enough to store it."*

The word tithe means a tenth. In practice, it is simply to donate or give one-tenth of all your income to the house of the Lord. The missionary who introduced me to Christ also introduced me to this principle. I immediately started practicing this principle from age fifteen, when I gave my heart to Jesus Christ, and the year the Lord blessed me with my first job. Though there were times when I wasn't as consistent as I wanted to be and should have been, I continue to put that principle into practice to this day. When the principle was introduced to me, I interpreted it literally, as I would still say we could in most cases. The practical application for me then was that as soon as I started working, I should not hesitate, waver or question the command of God. I was taught that delayed obedience translates into disobedience. The scriptures also warn against double-mindedness, which could result in forfeiting the abundant blessings of God.

I immediately started giving one-tenth of my monthly income, which was $11.60, to the church I attended. Compared to today, this amount was very little; you may say it was next to nothing. But for me, giving that amount at that time was a huge sacrifice. By the time I met my financial obligations (paid my bills), I had less than five dollars left. I had no money for the luxuries of life, such as entertainment, material things, or traveling, and I could not invest or save, but I was used to that because I came from humble beginnings. For four years, I wore the same skirt and the same three white blouses to school. I wore out one side of the skirt, and when the color faded, my grandmother turned it on the other side, and I continued wearing it. By the time I graduated, my blouses were no longer white. It is amazing the lessons of resilience one can learn from life's challenges. One of those lessons is to honor God with all He has blessed you with by being grateful, and I was grateful for that first job. It was a privilege for me to be able to give to the Lord.

For years I had nothing more than my monthly salary to live on, but I could see the hand of the Lord in everything I did, so I continued tithing. Not only was I tithing, but I started combining tithing with giving, praying, and fasting. I began to be intentional about giving. I started looking for opportunities to give in to the Kingdom as well. I gave to all kinds of Kingdom projects, including building fund projects. I gave to missions and missionaries. I looked for ways to bless the leaders of the churches I attended.

As I tithed, I continued to experience more and more financial blessings over the years. As I continued to tithe and give into the Kingdom, God gave me amazing favors. He opened doors of opportunities for me, some of which I mentioned throughout this book. Others will be for another book. However, let me share with you at least one of those opportunities to appreciate how faithful God is to His word and how important it is to be obedient to His word and live a life of integrity.

I lived in Latin America with my husband and son, where my husband was serving as a diplomat. The Lord continued to bless us both financially more and more. He and I were now earning more than we ever did before. Our financial investments were also doing quite well, and I was tithing from my salary, but I did"t tithe on my husband's salary. Although I had the liberty to spend from both our incomes without reservation or hesitation, for some reason, it never occurred to me to tithe from his income as well, not to mention tithing on our investment income. I just didn't think I could.

One day, I heard the voice of the Lord quite clearly asking me why I was not tithing on my husband's income. I quickly responded that I could not because the money was my husband's; it was not mine. In order to tithe from his salary, I would have to ask him for permission, especially since it was so much. He would never give that amount of money to the church. In my mind, when I did the math, that was too much money, and since I had never given so much money to a church before, it was simply inconceivable. *How could I?* These were my emotionalized thoughts – I was afraid to give so much.

Upon reflection, I think I was unwilling to give so much. It was easy to give $100 of the $1,000 I was earning, but $650? That was simply too much. I told myself my husband would never agree to that, and if I were to do that without asking him, he would be furious. Then I heard the Lord say to me, "A very convenient response. How about when you go shopping at La Gloria? Don't you use his money? You don't have to ask his permission to buy those expensive bags, shoes, and dresses." I knew that the Lord was right, and I knew what I had to do. This was the moment of truth, and I had to obey. I felt in my heart that I would tell my husband what I planned to do. I was doubtful he would agree, but I needed to. I felt my heart racing in my chest just thinking of what that would mean for me.

I don't remember whether I asked him for permission or used the privilege and simply wrote the first cheque for $650.00 but in obedience to the Lord, I took the cheque to church with me that Sunday. When it was time to give in the offering, the closer the offering basket came to me, the more my heart pounded. I clearly remember how difficult it was to drop the cheque in the offering. We were worshiping as the ushers collected the Lord's tithes and offerings as we usually did, and I was singing harder and lifted my hands higher to distract me from the struggle that was taking place inside me. *Should I or shouldn't I? My God, this is too difficult,* I thought.

When the basket was handed to me, I gently placed the cheque in it with trembling hands. My eyes were closed, and I was still worshiping and singing. At that moment, my worship went to a whole other level and took on a whole other meaning. I felt the joy of the Lord. *I am going to receive manifold financial blessings,* I thought, *the Lord is going to bless me financially as He promised He would in Malachi 3:10.* At that moment, the voice of the Lord said to me, "I will let you see souls come into the Kingdom." I was angry, and I responded in my heart, *Souls Lord? What am I going to do with souls?*

What a promise! That was not what I wanted to hear from the Lord, though. I wanted to hear Him confirm what I was thinking. I wanted to hear Him say how he would make me rich and add no sorrow, as the Bible says. I wanted to hear Him tell me He would give me blessings pressed down and running over as the Bible promises in Luke 6:38. But, here He was telling me He was going to bless me by letting me experience souls coming into the Kingdom.

I didn't know at that time the Lord was rewarding me with what He rewarded Jesus, the restoration of the souls of mankind. Jesus died for man to be restored to God; He had to shed His blood, I didn't. All I needed to do was tell mankind the good news of the gospel, and I would see souls come into the Kingdom. The scriptures say that "He who wins souls is wise." (Proverbs 11:30 NIV). I did not realize that God was promising me what He promised King Solomon. He gave Solomon wisdom and riches. My God, what an honor!

I wish I could tell you that I immediately pursued souls for the Kingdom. But, as I grew in the Lord, I began to feel the stirring in my heart to pray for souls to come into the Kingdom, and I started praying for the desire to win souls to Christ so I could experience that amazing promise of God. Years later, after graduating from Bible school, I felt the anointing of God upon my life to win souls. I have since had the privilege not only of leading souls to Christ, but I continue to pray for those who will come to the altar to give their lives to Christ. I also have the privilege of being able to disciple and mentor many young people as they begin their journey of a life with Christ.

God continued to shower financial blessings on my family and me. In addition to the financial blessings, He favored me with spiritual blessings. He has blessed me with an understanding of His Word and the gift of giving. He blessed me with the gift of understanding how to trade in stocks and options on the stock market. He gave me the desire to get involved in real estate sales and blessed me so much that I became one of the top sales agents in my office. He also blessed me with knowledge and understanding of real estate investments; I began to buy and sell both new and used homes. I would purchase homes from counties, refurbish them, and sell them at no less than a 20% return on my investment. Today, I mentor and coach leaders in the Kingdom of God on applying Biblical principles for financial prosperity and success.

In addition to these amazing blessings I received from God as a result of honoring him with tithes and offerings, God has also blessed me with the gift of wisdom. I was not aware of it until quite later in life. One of the comments I always hear from people is that I am a woman of great wisdom and humility. At first, it sounded strange to hear that comment from my peers and professors in graduate school. I didn't believe it at first; I thought they were just being kind and couldn't find anything else to compliment me with. When we were giving feedback to each other, my feedback was always that I was so wise. However, since I hear it more frequently from people in all environments that I frequent, I thank God for giving me more than I asked for that day at church when I gave Him that first big tithe cheque. Since then, I have given hundreds of thousands of dollars in tithes and offerings to the Lord. I know that it is because I gave that first cheque of $11.60. Today, the least I give to the expansion of the Kingdom of God is a tenth. God's faithfulness and goodness inspire me at times to give much more than a tenth of all He has blessed me with.

Let me stop here to say that my interpretation of this scripture today is different from what it used to be at age 15. When the principle was introduced to me, I interpreted it literally as in most cases we should. I have come to understand that all that the Lord has blessed me with, not only financially, belongs to Him. At least one-tenth of all that God has blessed you with, your time, your treasure, and your talent is to expand the Kingdom of God. Being obedient to God with our resources is a true demonstration of our commitment to its expansion.

If you find that you are struggling with your obedience in the area of tithing, you are not alone. The good news is that the Divine Coach can help you here as well. This is one of the amazing benefits of our divine partnership with Him. The only way we will not receive His help is if we are not willing to obey Him or if we intentionally disobey His leading and guidance. Doing so will definitely quench or silence his voice. In the next section, we discuss how we silence Him and some tips on how to avoid silencing Him.

Disobedience Quenches The Voice of the Divine Coach

Many believers struggle with the concept of quenching the Divine Coach. They confuse the unpardonable sin with quenching Him, but the two are not the same. Just to clarify what the unpardonable sin is for those of you who may be hearing about this theological concept for the first time. In Thessalonians 5:19, the Apostle Paul warned us about the possibility of quenching the Divine Coach by committing the unpardonable sin.

To put it into immediate context, Jesus is the one who first brought this theological concept to our awareness. Jesus had just performed a miracle which prompted opposition from the Pharisees who were present that day. Matthew 12:22-24 records that a demon-possessed man who was "blind, and dumb" was brought to the Lord. Since He was the Son of God and Israel's Messiah, the Lord had authority over both the supernatural and physical realms. Therefore, He simply cast out the demon and healed the man so that he could see and speak. This amazed the people who saw the miracle, and they wondered out loud, "Is this not the son of David?" – meaning Israel's long-promised Messiah and King. Hearing the crowd say this, Christ's enemies reacted: *"But when the Pharisees heard it, they said, This fellow doth not cast out devils, but by Beelzebub the prince of the devils."*

Christ had just freed this man from the grip and bondage of Satan right before their eyes. You would think that this would have been a moment of rejoicing over the healing of the man who had just been freed from the demon and could speak and see. Instead, the unbelieving Pharisees were infuriated. They could not deny the miracle, so they tried to explain it away by attributing it to Satan. They would not allow themselves to believe the possibility that Jesus of Nazareth was the King, the Son of David, so they attributed the miracle to another ruler, claiming that the Lord did it by the power of Beelzebub, the prince of the devils, which is Satan.

The Lord, in turn, addressed their unbelief and this accusation, telling them, *"And if Satan cast out Satan, he is divided against himself; how shall then his kingdom stand?"* The Lord advanced His wise argument a step further when He asked, *"Or else, how can one enter into a strong man's house, and spoil his goods, except he first binds the strong man? and then he will spoil his house."* In this verse, the "strong man" is Satan. His "house" is the world because Satan, according to 2 Corinthians 4:4, "is the god of this world." "His goods" are his demons and their evil works. Christ is the One who came from heaven and entered the world, the strong man's house, bound the strong man, plundered his goods, and cast out a demon. Christ did not perform this miracle in the power of Satan; Christ is not subject to him. Therefore, the logical conclusion is that Christ is greater and more powerful than the strong man, Satan, because Christ is God, and He demonstrated it by casting out one of Satan's demons.

I know this theological concept may sound scary to most believers, but there is no need to be afraid. As Gentiles or non-Jewish believers in Christ Jesus, we need to note to whom the Lord is speaking. First, He is specifically addressing Israel's unbelieving religious leaders. Accusing Christ of being in league with Satan and casting out a demon in the power of Satan was blasphemy to these religious leaders. Blasphemy is something that is done or said against God. By declaring that what they had just accused Him of was blasphemy, Christ affirmed His Deity, that He is God Almighty.

From a theological standpoint, it is important to bear in mind who Jesus was addressing at that time. The Gospel records that Christ was speaking to Israel. This is made obvious a few chapters later where the Lord said, "I am not sent but unto the lost sheep of the house of Israel" (Matt. 15:24). In Romans 15:8, Paul wrote, "Now I say that Jesus Christ was a minister of the circumcision [the Jews] for the truth of God, to confirm the promises made unto the fathers." Christ was sent to and ministered to Israel. In the Gospels, during the Lord's earthly ministry, you find Him ministering the truth of God and confirming the promises made to the fathers, Abraham, Isaac, and Jacob, according to the law, Israel's covenants, and prophecy.

Israel's accusation, therefore, of Christ casting out demons by the power of Satan did not make any sense and, thus, was egregious and unpardonable for two reasons: first, they were admitting that Satan was working against himself by relinquishing control of someone in his clutches and then turning around and repairing the damage. That did not make any sense. Second, likening the work of the Holy Spirit in the life of Christ as Satanic was egregious because these religious leaders knew better. They just refused to believe that Jesus was the Messiah sent to deliver Israel from their sin and reconcile them to God. How could He be? In their opinion, nothing good could come out of Nazareth, and Jesus was a Nazarene. Jesus knew that this was their reasoning, and that is why He told them that they could not be pardoned for likening the work of the Holy Spirit of God, which was evident in their eyes, as satanic.

Rejection of the Holy Spirit Automatically Quenches Him

Israel rejected Jesus, and in turn, they rejected the Holy Spirit. The Holy Spirit was their last chance to repent, believe, and be saved. That's why blaspheming the third person of the Trinity was unforgivable. The Holy Spirit came at Pentecost (Acts 2:1-4) and then worked mightily in Israel with signs and wonders. Those signs and wonders, done in the name of Jesus Christ, confronted Israel and its leaders with overwhelming proof of Christ's resurrection and Messiahship (Acts 3:6-21).

Blaspheming the Spirit in deliberate rebellion completely rejects Him as an integral part of the Godhead in totality, but Israel decided to reject Him anyway, and, by their own choice, they forfeited their opportunity to be reconciled to God. Still, today, when Christ is presented to the world, and people reject Him, they refuse the opportunity to be reconciled to God.

When we accept Jesus Christ as Savior, it takes submission to and obedience to the voice of the Holy Spirit. By the very act of saying "yes" to Christ, you are saying "yes" to the Holy Spirit. God in His mercy makes it possible for us to say "yes" to Jesus by causing the Spirit to move upon our hearts. Philippians 2:13 confirms that the Holy Spirit moves in our hearts, empowering us to say "yes," and it is God's amazing grace towards us.

But God's Grace is Greater Than All Our Sin

We live under a different program now, separate from the program that was suspended because of the unpardonable sin. The unpardonable sin cannot be committed under grace. That warning from Christ was for Israel and its religious leaders. Its dispensational context was that of Israel's prophetic program and the coming of the Holy Spirit to Israel. It had to do with Israel's rejection of Christ and the ministry of the Holy Spirit to Israel. The unpardonable sin does not apply to us today, nor has it applied to anyone since the stoning of Stephen. God has rendered it impossible to commit this sin today because His program changed from Israel to the Body of Christ. Thus, when we rightly divide God's Word, the unforgivable sin does not need to strike fear in our hearts.

Also, to suggest that the omnipotent Spirit of God could ever be quenched, and thus restricted in what He might do in the lives of believers today, is to tread on thin theological ice. As non-Jewish believers or Gentiles, we are under grace, unlike Israel, who was under the law. Therefore, it is critically important to keep in mind whenever you read and study the four Gospels that there are promises of blessing and punishment made to Israel that are not for us today under grace, such as blasphemy against the Holy Spirit and the unpardonable sin.

In 1 Thessalonians 5, Paul says that God has granted believers the ability to restrict or release what the Spirit does in their lives. The Divine

Coach comes to us like a fire, either to be fanned into full flame and given the freedom to accomplish His will or to be doused and extinguished by the water of human fear, control, and even flawed theology. All the Holy Spirit, your Divine Coach, wants to do is intensify the heat of His presence in you. He wants to inflame your hearts and fill you with the warmth of His indwelling power so that instead of committing the unpardonable sin or even risking quenching Him, you will be empowered by His presence.

As believers in Christ Jesus, it is important to note that although we may not commit the unpardonable sin by deliberately rejecting God the Holy Spirit, it is equally important for you to know that you have the power and authority to release, restrict or even inadvertently quench what the Holy Spirit can do in your life. Since partnering with the Divine Coach is critical to obtaining His support, the one thing you do not want to do is to quench Him by disobeying Him when He speaks to you. There are several ways in which you can quench the effectiveness of the Divine Coach. In the following section, I discuss five ways in which you can unknowingly quench the work of the Divine Coach in your life.

Five Ways We Can Unknowingly Quench the Divine Coach

1. **We quench the Spirit whenever we diminish His personality and speak of Him as if He were only an abstract power or source of divine energy.**

    Some believers speak of the Divine Coach as if He was no more than an ethereal energy, the divine equivalent to an electric current. We fail to honor His exalted status as God, and we fail to embrace His sovereignty over us. The result is that when anyone confirms hearing His voice or experiencing Him in any way, it is summarily dismissed as dishonoring His exalted status as God and a failure to embrace His sovereignty over us rather than ours over Him.

2. **We quench the voice of the Divine Coach when we ignore His voice.**

When you intentionally and decisively ignore the counsel of the Holy Spirit, seek out human counsel, and rely on any resource other than the Holy Spirit for anything you do in life, you dishonor Him. This is self-reliance or trusting in man rather than trusting in God. In doing so, you run the risk of never hearing his voice in your life again – you will quench Him. Eli, his sons, and King Saul suffered that consequence in the Old Testament. God rejected Eli and his sons and chose Samuel to replace them. He rejected King Saul and replaced him with David. The one thing you do not want to risk is being replaced by God. When He calls you, be ready to go with Him all the way to the end of your life and do so, relying only on His guidance and direction through the Holy Spirit.

God does not want you to rely on yourself to do His will. He wants to partner with you through His Spirit to accomplish His divine plan for your life. In Romans 15:13, Paul warns against self-reliance. He cautions us that any attempt on our part to conjure up hope apart from the power which comes only from the Divine Coach is to silence or quench Him. According to Colossians 1:29, Paul encourages us to depend only on Christ's mighty power to work within us as we fulfill our divine calling. It is only through the power of the Divine Coach you can effectively fulfill your unique divine calling in the Kingdom of God. Any effort to carry out your functions other than through the energy that He powerfully works within you will quench the Divine Coach. In essence, 2 Thessalonians 1:11 confirms that any attempt you make to resolve or carry out some good work of faith through a power other than the Divine Coach is to quench Him.

3. **The Holy Spirit is the Spirit of Prophecy. We quench Him whenever we dishonor or despise prophetic utterances.**

Prophecy is a gift from God to believers. In 1 Thessalonians 5:19-20, Paul warns in this way, "Do not quench the Spirit. Do not despise prophecies, but test everything; hold fast what is good." Prophetic utterances are God's way of communicating to believers through His Holy Spirit. He uses men and women who have what we know as the gift of prophecy. Through prophecy, God reveals to us the present and future operations in the realm of the supernatural where He dwells.

Prophecy, therefore, should not be despised because to do so is to despise God Himself and the word of God.

However, the gift of prophecy has been so abused that most believers do not appreciate its relevance and importance.

According to the scriptures, it is the highest or most important gift we have received from God. No matter how badly the gift of prophecy may have been abused and despised, according to the scriptures, it is a sin to despise prophetic utterances.

God commands us not to treat prophecy with contempt, as if it were unimportant. Prophetic utterances are the voice of the Holy Spirit Himself. Treating the prophetic utterances of the Holy Spirit with scorn and contempt is one way in which you can guarantee that you will quench Him.

Rather than quenching the Holy Spirit by despising prophetic utterances, Paul tells us in 1 Thessalonians 5:21 to "test everything," meaning examine or judge all prophecies. Paul doesn't correct the abuse of this gift by commending disuse (as is the practice of many today). Instead, his remedy is biblically informed discernment and only "holding fast to what is good." Such discernment should be applied to all spiritual gifts.

4. **We quench the work of the Divine Coach by diminishing the importance and the relevance of His divine activity among us.**

The Holy Spirit's operations among us are what alerts and awakens us to the glorious and majestic truth that we are truly the children of God. In Romans 8:15–16 and Galatians 4:4–7, Paul discusses the experiential assurance of our adoption as the children of God, which He explains is the direct result of the work of the Divine Coach in our hearts. To whatever extent believers diminish this experiential dimension of the Divine Coach's work, they quench Him.

5. **Suppressing our emotions in praise and worship quenches Him**.

One of the ways we experience the presence of the Divine Coach within is through our powerful emotions. One such emotion is joy, which I mentioned above. It is the manifestation of His presence in our life. Jesus, as He extolled the Father, is described as rejoicing "in the Holy Spirit" (Luke 10:21). Affections for God such as joy, peace, love, zeal, desire, and reverential fear are essential dimensions in Christ-exalting worship. John Piper, founder and teacher of desiringgod.org says it best: "The vibrant fullness of the Spirit overflows in appropriate expressions like singing and making melody from the heart to the Lord (Ephesians 5:18-19). And, if you don't like those expressions and you resist it, fold your arms or say in your heart, 'I am not going to do that sort of thing; I am not going to sing you are quenching the Holy Spirit.'"

To suppress our heartfelt affections and emotions or even to have those emotions legislated in any way and in any environment, whether it be in corporate gatherings, where strict guidelines as to how you should worship are issued, is one of the most common ways in which the Holy Spirit is inadvertently quenched in our lives. As believers, we should guard vigilantly against doing it intentionally or having it legislated to us.

As you read these five ways in which you can quench the powerful move of the Divine Coach within, I urge you to carefully search your own heart and assess the possible ways in which you may have quenched the Spirit in your own life and in the experience of your local church? Yielding to and making room for the operation of the Divine Coach in our midst is not to be feared but fostered. May God grant us the wisdom and confidence in His goodness to facilitate a greater and more life-changing experience of the Divine Coach's transforming power.

CHAPTER VIII

Accessing The Help of the Divine Coach

Being Born Again Gives Us Immediate Access to the Help of the Divine Coach

The Divine Coach desires to reconcile us to God so that we can have a relationship with Him that is real and personal. Reconciliation to God is what is referred to in the scriptures as salvation, and it is the first step to having access to the help of the Divine Coach.

There is no salvation or relationship with God without the Holy Spirit. It is completely unbiblical to suggest that someone could enter into a relationship with Christ without the intervention of the Holy Spirit. Jesus said that it is by the Spirit that we are born-again unto new life.

At the moment of our salvation, the Spirit takes up permanent residence in us to teach and guide us into all truth. Romans 8:14-16 says, "For as many as are led *(present tense –being led)* by the Spirit of God, they are the sons of God. For ye have not received the spirit of bondage again to fear; but ye have received the Spirit of adoption, whereby we cry, Abba, Father. The Spirit itself beareth witness with our spirit, that we are the children of God." Once we are reconciled to God, we are granted immediate access to the help of the Divine Coach. It is a gift of God that He promised to our children and us so that we can know the mind of Christ and the amazing plans that He has for our lives.

Once that access is granted, the Divine Coach takes up His primary role as intermediary or mediator between God and us, revealing all divine truth. The Divine Coach, being the intermediary in the Godhead, is referred to as the Spirit of truth.One of His roles is to communicate truth to the believer. In this divine partnership with us, He communicates the all-important truth about who God is, who we are, and our life purpose. As our helper, He must have immediate access at all times to all wisdom, knowledge, and understanding of the Godhead. Being an integral part of the Godhead is the only way He can effectively help us.

Jesus speaking to His disciples in John 16:13 confirms, "He [the Divine Coach] will only speak what He hears. He will tell you what is yet to come." In doing so, He will perform one of His most important functions, which is to allow us access to the truth of our identity in Christ Jesus and empower us to bring glory to God. "He will bring glory to Me by taking from what is Mine and making it known to you," and further "… all that belongs to the Father is Mine." These all-important truth messages do not come from our external environment. They come from the Holy Spirit, who communicates truth to you to help you live a victorious life.

In 1 Corinthians 2:12-16, the scripture clarifies some of the key roles of the Divine Coach in our lives, the most important of which is to give access into the mind of Christ. This access gives us an advantage over the devil as he does not know the mind of Christ; only the Holy Spirit does. We will always need divine help as long as there are challenges and adversities in this world. We can rest assured that we'll always have access to His help when they come our way.

First, as believers, we need to know that we have received the Spirit from God. He was given to us so that, according to 1 Corinthians 2:12, we may understand what God has freely given us. Secondly, the Divine Coach helps us by revealing the thoughts of God to us. Knowing God so intimately (He knows the thoughts of God and searches them (v.10 & 11)) and accessing His help provides us with divine revelation and understanding of the immense unlimited divine power residing within us. *Paul confirms in verse* 13 *that* we speak what we receive from the Spirit, not our assumptions but divine revelations directly from the Spirit. Our role is not only to obey, but as salt and light to the world, we are to communicate the all-important message of reconciliation to God. One of the things we must remember, though, is that because these messages *"are spiritually discerned"* (v.14), the world will not receive them. However, because *"we have the mind of Christ"* (v.16), we will be able to access, receive and understand the revelations of the Divine Coach.

In 1 Corinthians 2:10 - 13, Paul shares how the Divine Coach, the Holy Spirit, helps us.

He does so by searching all things in heaven and on earth, things that the ordinary person will never know, giving us divine wisdom, revelation, and discernment, helping us make informed, wise choices and respond appropriately to life challenges and adversities.

> *"The Spirit searches all things, even the deep things of God. For who among men knows the thoughts of man except his own spirit within him? So too, no one knows the thoughts of God except the Spirit of God. We have not received the spirit of the world, but the Spirit who is from God, that we may understand what God has freely given us. And this is what we speak, not in words taught us by human wisdom, but in words taught by the Spirit, expressing spiritual truths in spiritual words. The natural man does not accept the things that come from the Spirit of God. For they are foolishness to him, and he cannot understand them because they are spiritually discerned. The spiritual man judges all things, but he himself is not subject to anyone's judgment. For who has known the mind of the Lord, so as to instruct Him?" But we have the mind of Christ*
>
> *(1 Corinthians 2:10-16 NSB).*

We can only know the mind of Christ as believers by communicating directly with Him in prayer, which is one of the major ways our Divine Coach helps us with life challenges and adversities.

We Access The Help of The Divine Coach When we Pray

God loves us so much that He wants us to succeed in all we do. In order to ensure that success, He has given us direct access to Him day and night through the Divine Coach. This direct communication line allows us to communicate with Him and to receive messages from Him. This is what we call prayer. Prayer is direct communication to God. When we receive the gift of salvation, we are also given another gift, the Holy Spirit. We are His children, and as children, we should have access to our Father. We have access to our earthly fathers directly, don't we?

God does not want us to hear from anyone else if He can prevent it. He prefers to speak to us directly, so He has established this spiritual communication channel with Him, which we call prayer. Jesus, speaking to His disciples before He left them, reassures them of the importance of asking for and receiving His help in prayer. "*In that day, you will not [need to] ask Me about anything. I assure you and most solemnly say to you, whatever you ask the Father in My name [as My representative], He will give you.*" *(John 16:23 AMP)* As believers, this *is* your invitation to access the Holy Spirit's help. You must not hesitate to pray. Let me encourage you to reach out to God in prayer consistently when you need His help. It is one of the privileges you have as a child of God.

Jesus, knowing the importance of consistent prayer to access divine help, encourages His disciples in this way, "Men ought always to pray and faint not." He does so by providing the following illustration of how persistent prayer gives access to God's help in Luke 18 verse 1 which is still relevant to us, as His followers, today.

"There was a judge in a certain city," he said, *"who neither feared God nor cared about people. A widow of that city came to him repeatedly, saying, 'Give me justice in this dispute with my enemy.' The judge ignored her for a while, but finally he said to himself, 'I don't fear God or care about people, but this woman is driving me crazy. I'm going to see that she gets justice, because she is wearing me out with her constant requests! Then the Lord said, "Learn a lesson from this unjust judge. Even he rendered a just decision in the end. So don't you think God will surely give justice to his chosen people who cry out to him day and night? Will he keep putting them off? I tell you, he will grant justice to them quickly! But when the Son of Man returns, how many will he find on the earth who have faith?"*

(Luke 18:2-8 NLT)

Notice the question Jesus asked the disciples, *"When the Son of Man returns, how many will he find on the earth who has faith?"* This suggests that it does not only take humility to go to God in prayer – it also takes faith to pray so that you can access the help of the Divine Coach. So, let me ask you, how would you respond if Jesus had posed that question to you? Would He find faith in you when He returns to the earth? Fortunately, He is so mindful that this faith is not humanly achieved that He made sure that each believer received this divine gift so we can get the help we need to pray effectively. Yes, faith is the gift we receive through the Holy Spirit to pray effectively.

We Access The Help Of The Divine Coach As We Pray Effectively

The Divine Coach is our perfect prayer partner. He was sent to teach us how to pray when we are weak, fearful, feeling inadequate, and condemned in the presence of God because of our humanity and thus unable to articulate what is deep within our souls. During this time, the Divine Coach takes an active part in our prayer lives, empowering us to pray according to the will of God and not our own will. To accurately discern the will of God, we need the help of the Divine Coach to help us to pray effectively. James 5:16 says that the effectual fervent prayer of the righteous avails much. This means that we can pray effectively or ineffectively when we try to access the Divine Coach's help. Sometimes when I go to pray, I am not in the right spirit. This happens especially when I am tired from a stressful day at work, when there is some challenge in my life, or when there's some sin in my life. As soon as I start to pray, I become conscious of my physical, emotional or spiritual state. Sometimes I begin to condemn myself for the terribleness of my sin as I go into the presence of God and start to pray.

Sometimes Satan tries to use a shortcoming, weakness, or habit as a stronghold in my life. That life challenge at times becomes such a burden on my heart, and though I know that I should ask for the help of the Divine Coach, in my humanity, my ego sometimes gets the better of me, and I don't want to. However, when I humble myself with the help of the Divine Coach, I am able to put aside my fear and ego and yield to the Lord in prayer.

The Divine Coach empowers me to bow my will before God and seek His help. In almost every prayer I pray, the Spirit has to encourage me to remove myself, submit to God, resist the Devil, and he will flee from me. Prayer is one of the ways we partner with the Divine Coach to come to know, perceive and understand the will of God. In so doing, we also partner in the delivery of His will. More importantly, we access His help to deal with whatever challenge or adversity we face.

We Access The Help of Our Divine Coach Only After We have Been Born Again

The Divine Coach is our perfect prayer partner because He desires to make our relationship with God real and personal. There is no salvation or relationship with God without the Holy Spirit. It is completely unbiblical to suggest that someone could enter into a relationship with Christ without the intervention of the Holy Spirit. Jesus said that it is by the Spirit that we are born-again unto new life. At the moment of our salvation, the Spirit takes up permanent residence in us to teach and guide us into all truth. Romans 8:14-16 says, "For as many as are led *(present tense –being led)* by the Spirit of God, they are the sons of God. For ye have not received the spirit of bondage again to fear; but ye have received the Spirit of adoption, whereby we cry, Abba, Father. The Spirit itself beareth witness with our spirit, that we are the children of God.

God wants you to recognize the voice of the Holy Spirit and be obedient to Him. This means you and I are not here on our own to do just whatever pleases us in this world. God is counting on us to do what He tells us and to go where He sends us. He wants us to stay in an environment where He can use us effectively. As His messengers, He wants us to communicate His messages accurately so that the world can know His heart's desires. In essence, He wants you and me to be His ambassadors here in this earth realm, and the only way we can carry out and fulfill that mandate to His satisfaction is in partnership with His Holy Spirit, our Divine Coach.

God's heartfelt desire is to clearly communicate His will and purpose for us. Jesus assured us while He was here on the earth that His only reason for coming to the earth was to give us life and that we experience that life to its fullness. According to Matthew 7:14, Jesus came that we might comprehend what it means to walk the narrow road and go through the small gate that leads to life. He demonstrated that abundant life in partnership with the Holy Spirit. It was only through that divine partnership with the Divine Coach that His life was able to manifest miracles, signs, and wonders. And it is only through that divine partnership that you will be able to do greater works than the ones Jesus did while He was here as noted in Philippians 2:13: "For it is God Who works in you to will and to act according to His good purpose."

So, what qualifications do we bring to this partnership? Are we mortals able to partner with divinity to expand the Kingdom of God, thereby experiencing the abundant life we desire on this earth realm? Yes, we are because God has given us the capacity to hear from the Divine Coach and work with Him to accomplish His divine purposes on earth, but He will never force us into that partnership.

We have to want that partnership, ask for it and maintain it. The partnership is reciprocal, and it is based solely on the exercise of our free will. God has given men and women a free will to choose how they live their lives. He gave it to Adam and Eve, and He gave it to us. We have the free will to choose how much of God to allow or not to allow into our lives.

The most important gift that God has given us is a free will. He desires that we respond to Him, bringing ourselves into agreement with Him, to accomplish His divine plan for our lives wherever we go. To accomplish His divine plans, He desires for us to follow the guidance of the Divine Coach by submitting the members of our bodies as instruments of righteousness so that His will can be known and manifested through us throughout the entire earth. Submitting in prayer is one of the most effective and powerful ways in which believers can accomplish this.

We Access The Divine Coach's Helps Through Fasting

Another effective way mentioned in the scriptures to access the help of the Divine Coach is by submitting the members of your body as instruments of righteousness to God. We do that through the method of fasting. People who take prayer seriously know how powerful fasting is, but what about missing meals that make prayer so potent?

Fasting is known to touch the heart of God where prayer alone can't. So, what is fasting? Is it a form of hunger strike, blackmailing God like a spoiled child holding its breath until it's blue and gets what it wants? Obviously not! What is it about fasting that touches the heart of God? Jesus first mentioned prayer combined with fasting in the New Testament.

The disciples had seen and heard Jesus' prayers on many occasions. They had also witnessed many miracles after He prayed. He had prayed a powerful prayer to God the Father on one such occasion, affirming that He knew that His Father always hears Him when He prays. Immediately following that affirmation, He ordered Lazarus out of the grave.

Instantly, Lazarus, who was dead for four days, emerged alive from the grave. So the disciples knew that prayer was powerful. They had even asked Jesus to teach them how to pray. Obviously, they wanted to experience the same power of God when they prayed, and they did. They came back from a mission trip once and boasted to Jesus about how successful the trip was. They told Him that even the demons were subject to them. However, one day, they tried to cast out a demon, but to their consternation, the demon did not obey. They were confused, and then Jesus used the opportunity to teach them another powerful spiritual principle by telling them, "These kinds do not go out except by prayer and fasting."

Jesus had given them some important guidelines about fasting, one of which was to fast in secret, and the other was not to boast about fasting. Perhaps this was the opportune moment for Jesus to address their attitude when they returned from that mission trip. They came back so elated that the demons were subject to them, they most likely displayed arrogance. Who really knows? Jesus, however, had to caution them to remember that they were dealing with powerful demons and that prayer alone would not always suffice. There was a powerful combination that demons bowed to and that was fasting combined with prayer. Jesus needed them to be aware of that powerful combination.

I believe that Jesus wanted to hand down this powerful spiritual principle to us as well. So when the religious leaders asked Him why John's disciples fasted and not His, He told them something very interesting. He said that fasting was unnecessary while He was on the earth, but they would fast when He returned to heaven.

You see, the people of Israel were living a life that was displeasing to God even up to the time of Jesus. Yet, they continued with their religious practices, one of which was fasting. Despite their insensitive and selfish lifestyles, they expected that God would have been pleased with them. But, as you can see in the following account found in the book of Isaiah, God was not pleased with their behavior, so He rejected their fasting.

There is only one type of fast mentioned in God's Word as approved by and pleasing to God. Here are His sentiments as recorded in Isaiah 58:1-8:

> *"Shout it aloud, do not hold back. Raise your voice like a trumpet. Declare to my people their rebellion and to the descendants of Jacob their sins. For day after day they seek me out; they seem eager to know my ways as if they were a nation that does what is right and has not forsaken the commands of its God.*

> *They ask me for a just decision and seem eager for God to come near them. 'Why have we fasted,' they say, 'and you have not seen it? Why have we humble ourselves and you have not noticed? "Yet on the day of your fasting, you do as you please and exploit all your workers. Your fasting ends in quarreling and strife, and in striking each other with wicked fists. You cannot fast as you do today and expect your voice to be heard on high. Is this the kind of fast I have chosen, only a day for people to humble themselves? Is it only for bowing one's head like a reed and for lying in sackcloth and ashes? Is that what you call a fast, a day acceptable to the Lord? "Is not this the kind of fasting I have chosen: to lose the chains of injustice and untie the cords of the yoke, to set the oppressed free and break every yoke?*

> *Is it not to share your food with the hungry and to provide the poor wanderer with shelter- when you see the naked, to clothe them, and not to turn away from your own flesh and blood? Then your light will break forth like the dawn, and your healing will quickly appear; then your righteousness[a] will go before you, and the glory of the Lord will be your rear guard."*

Evidently, the above specifics of fasting is the type of fast God approved for the children of Israel, and I will dare say that it brings us specific benefits and outcomes even for us today. This fast empowers us, brings us joy, satisfies our every need, brings answers to our prayers, and reveals us as children of righteousness in this dark world. This type of fast not only benefits us as individuals but it brings the blessings of God to our nation.

The following are two biblical examples of how fasting combined with prayer brought the Divine Coach's guidance and intervention in the lives of the early believers:

Before Paul and Barnabas appointed elders in every church they fasted and prayed. *"With prayer and fasting, they turned the elders over to the care of the Lord, in whom they had put their trust." (Acts 14:23)*

> *"While fasting and praying the Holy Spirit confirmed the first special assignment God had for Paul and Barnabas. While they were worshiping the Lord and fasting, the Holy Spirit said, "Set apart for me Barnabas and Saul for the work to which I have called them." So after they had fasted and prayed, they placed their hands on them and sent them off. The two of them, sent on their way by the Holy Spirit, went down to Seleucia and sailed from there to Cyprus."*
>
> *(Acts 13:2-4)*

Indeed, when we fast, we must ensure that God accepts our fasting, or else not only are we angering God, we are fasting in vain. God does not always have to respond to our requests just because we fast. In times of unconfessed sin and disobedience, He doesn't respond to our prayers as we see in the life of David when he committed adultery with Bathsheba. David sought the Lord's mercy in prayer and fasting for the life of his and Bathsheba's child, but God did not respond to David because He was angry with him. In 2 Samuel 12:16, David pleaded with God for the child; he fasted and spent many nights lying in sackcloth on the ground. When David confessed his sin and repented before God, God pardoned and restored him, but He did not permit the child to live. Prayer alone is not enough in every situation. We must incorporate fasting with prayer to access the Holy Spirit's divine intervention. We must also not forget to confess and repent of our sins.

Repentance Combined with Fasting Gives Access to Increased Potential.

Once believers confess their sins, repent and incorporate fasting into their prayer life, they have access to an amazing potential that is not accessible through prayer alone. But in order for fasting to be effective, it must be combined with humility. The scriptures teach us that God resists the proud and gives grace to the humble. A sign of humility is to acknowledge when we have sinned. We do so by confessing that sin to God and asking Him to forgive us. "If we confess our sins, God is faithful and just to forgive us our sins and cleanse us from all unrighteousness." Fasting cannot be used as a manipulative spiritual strategy; God cannot be and will not be manipulated. If we expect to receive an answer to our prayers, we must examine ourselves to ensure that there is no unconfessed sin in our lives for which we need to repent, as in the case of David. Equally important is asking the person we have hurt to forgive us and whether the person forgives us is not important. Our duty is to forgive others and ask for forgiveness when we cause offense and hurt others. These are two steps we take to demonstrate a heart of humility. Repentance, on the other hand, goes a step further. We must stop doing what we have confessed and ask for God's forgiveness. These three steps combined are examples of humility and repentance. Here is what the Lord says in Joel 2:12-13, "Even now," declares the Lord, "return to me with all your heart, with fasting and weeping and mourning. Rend your heart and not your garments. Return to the Lord your God, for he is gracious and compassionate, slow to anger and abounding in love, and he relents from sending calamity." Rending your heart simply means that an outward show is not what God considers as humility. He desires a broken and contrite heart, as seen in the example I shared above in the life of David.

Another powerful example of true repentance and humility in the scriptures to support that repentance combined with fasting demonstrates a posture of humility before God, which resonates with me, is the one I read as a child, the story of Jonah and the Whale.

In Jonah chapter 3, the Bible says that the people of Nineveh were notorious for the terrible acts of atrocity they were committing against the surrounding nations. However, God loved them so much that He was willing to give them another chance to repent before He resorted to destroying the entire city. So He asked the Prophet Jonah to go to the city and preach the message of repentance so that the people would confess their sins and return to a lifestyle of righteousness. Jonah went reluctantly to the city of Nineveh to do God's bidding.

Jonah 3:5-9 states, "The Ninevites believed in God. A fast was proclaimed, and all of them, from the greatest to the least, put on sackcloth. When Jonah's warning reached the king of Nineveh, he rose from his throne, took off his royal robes, covered himself with sackcloth and sat down in the dust. This is the proclamation he issued in Nineveh. By the decree of the king and his nobles: Do not let people or animals, herds or flocks, taste anything; do not let them eat or drink. But let people and animals be covered with sackcloth. Let everyone call urgently on God. Let them give up their evil ways and their violence. Who knows? God may yet relent and with compassion turn from his fierce anger so that we will not perish." This outward posture of fasting and prayer demonstrated the Ninevites humility and obviously pleased God, so He responded by forgiving them. God will also respond not only by forgiving you but also empowering you to fulfill His divine plans when you demonstrate humility like the Ninevites did.

God loves you so much that He will never let sin stand in the way of forgiving you. He will always give you an opportunity to repent. To receive His forgiveness, you will need to respond by obeying the directive of the Holy Spirit. According to Psalm 145:8, God is slow to anger, rich in loving kindness and tender mercies, always abounding in love. His loving kindness and tender mercies manifested in His willingness to forgive are experienced when you repent. In order to repent, we need to have faith and believe that God will forgive us when we repent.

Fasting To Overcome Challenges and Adversities

Many believers fast to access the power of the Divine Coach so that they can overcome life's challenges and adversities. There are several other biblical reasons why one should engage in a personal fast. In Ezra 8:23, the people of God, "…fasted and petitioned God…" to overcome the challenges they were facing. In Nehemiah 1:4, Nehemiah testifies that he humbled himself and "fasted and prayed before the God of heaven." Having responded to God's call on his life, Nehemiah immediately started to face many difficult challenges which he knew he could not overcome without fasting and prayer. In his exile in Babylon, Daniel faced tremendous challenges at the hands of his peers and strengthened himself "…in prayer, petition, in fasting…" (Daniel 9:3) as he devoted himself to carrying out the will of God. Through fasting combined with prayer, both Nehemiah and Daniel accessed divine revelation and tremendous supernatural strength and deliverance, which enabled them to respond instead of reacting to the myriad of challenges and adversities they were facing.

Some believers fast because they believe that their fasting will cause God to hear them better somehow and that He would relent from His decisions. But, as I stated earlier, fasting is not a manipulative tool believers can use to get God's attention. Fasting does not change God's hearing, nor does it influence God to change His mind. God's Word is forever established in the heavens and nothing will cause Him to change His mind. For example, if an unrighteous person asks God during that fast to harm another person because they have been harmed, that is asking God to align His desires to ours. It will be chaotic in this world if God operates at the whim and fancy of everyone who fasts to get Him to do what they want. If, however, our petitions align with the will of God, then our fasting is not what causes

God to change His mind – instead, we would have tapped into His will, His commandments, and His righteous ways. Fasting does not change God as much as it changes our mindset and, ultimately, our praying.

There are several ways in which fasting changes our mindset and our prayers. Humans have a tendency to be self-reliant. We think that we do not need God. We become arrogant when we are in trouble and would rather go to another human to ask for help than humble ourselves and seek help from a God we cannot see or even hear from. In fact, in these contemporary times, speaking of God's existence or asking someone to seek help from a deity we cannot see when faced with life's challenges is a sign of weakness.

However, when a believer fasts, it demonstrates a changed mindset, one of humility. Your prayer life also changes. It shows that you are not leaning on your understanding anymore but that as a child of God, you depend on God for His divine intervention. When you fast, it heightens the seriousness of your prayers, and it creates a new level of urgency for God's answer.

When we are faced with life challenges and our minds are confused and we do not know how to respond, fasting brings us amazing clarity. I have lived a life of fasting and prayer. My experience when I fast is that it brings a greater sense of clarity and focus to my prayers, allowing me to respond appropriately to whatever the issue is that I brought to the Lord. It removes the focus from me and places it on God's ability to grant me the petition, according to His will, of course.

I have also noticed that I am no longer praying my imagination because of the absence of food in my system. I believe the Holy Spirit can get my attention much better, and I can hear His voice more clearly in that empty state.

Finally, my experience is that fasting leads to a deeper level of community with those who join us in our fasting and praying and communicates to God that our requests are urgent. As I write this chapter, I have been fasting for the past six weeks with a friend. Not only are we getting to know each other better, but I also observe that we are receiving responses to our prayer requests much faster. This could only mean that praying in a community communicates urgency to God. I truly believe that when two or three people or a group of people gather together in the name of the Lord, the Holy Spirit comes in our midst to help us with our petitions and God responds quickly.

Studying the Word of God

Romans 10:17 states, "So then faith cometh by hearing, and hearing by the word of God." Faith only comes when you hear the Word of God, and one of the best ways to hear the Word is when you set time aside to study the Word of God intentionally. Many believers possess a Bible, but some never take the time to open it, let alone read it. You see, it is not just enough to possess a Bible, you have to open it and read it to benefit from it. Reading the Bible is the first step to hearing and recognizing the voice of the Divine Coach, the Holy Spirit. This is how the partnership starts. A conversation must begin before a partnership can start.

The Divine Coach is the author of the Word of God. This can be seen in 2 Peter 1:21, "For prophecy never had its origin in the human will, but prophets, though human, spoke from God as they were carried along by the Holy Spirit." The Word is the manual that contains the blueprint and roadmap for our lives. However, having the Word of God available to us as children of God is not enough. We have to read and incorporate the Word into our daily life.

Priscilla Shirer tells the story of her dad, Dr. Tony Evans, and his relationship with technology. I will share the story with you to drive home the importance of the Word of God in our lives. Although Priscilla's father had many computers in his church office and home office, her dad never took the time to learn how to operate them. Up to this day, she says, her father still writes all of his sermons by hand using pen and yellow-lined notepaper.

However, one day, he just had to learn how to use the computer because he needed to get online to access his youngest son's college website. His son was playing on his school's sports team, and he wanted badly to watch his son play. This meant that he was forced to learn how to use the computer to access the internet to be able to watch the game. So, he called his daughter, Priscilla's younger sister, to ask for her help. The first thing she showed him was how to turn on the computer using the 'on' button. You may think this was pretty basic, but you must understand that her dad never turned on the computer.

Next, she proceeded to show him how to access the school's website. At which point the phone rang, and his daughter had to leave her father to answer the landline phone, which was in the kitchen. When she left the room, her father called out to her, "How do I find the webpage?" She responded to him from the kitchen and told him to use the mouse.

Now, dad did not know what the mouse was. So he began to look around on the desk until he saw this gadget which looked like something with a tail sticking out. Then he took it up and started rubbing it on the computer screen. When that did not work, he began to wave the mouse in the air, thinking it would bring him to the web page. What was the problem there? You guessed right, before this need arose to watch his son's game, he never even opened the computer he had for years let alone know how to navigate the web. The computers he owned remained unopened until something important enough to him like watching his son play made him desperate to learn how to use it. And so it is with the Word of God. We must open the Word of God daily because we cannot know the Word unless we read it often.

As believers, the Word of God is life to us. Jesus confirms to us that we cannot live our lives without the Word. It is the Word of God that helps us to walk in obedience to God. David exclaimed in Psalm 119:11, "Thy word have I hid in my heart, that I might not sin against thee." It is the Holy Spirit, our Divine Coach, that empowers us to understand the Word so that we can walk in obedience to it.

To honor the relationship we have with the Divine Coach, it is critical that we know and give attention to the Word of God. Obedience to the Word of God is the only way we can reap the benefits of our partnership with the Divine Coach. The Word of God is the covenant that He has established with believers. In Jeremiah 1:12, the Lord declares, "…for I am [actively] watching over my word to fulfill it." This implies that God never does anything outside of the covenant He established in His Word. God is faithful to His Word. His Word is Him, and He is His Word. He will not change His Word to meet our selfish needs, to fit into our busy schedules, or simply because we change our minds.

On the contrary, He will only answer us if we ask according to the promises and the covenants He has established in His Word.

God keeps His Word forever throughout all generations. David declares in Psalm 119:89, "Forever, O Lord, your word is firmly fixed in the heavens." This means that since God will only respond to what is in His Word, the believer must remember this important fact when partnering with the Divine Coach.

You Gain Access to the Divine Coach's Help by Incorporating the Word into Your Life

Apart from prayer and fasting, another way we access the help of the Divine Coach is by studying the Word and meditating on the word day and night. Being the author of the Word, the Divine Coach knows exactly what He wants to communicate to us. He wants to do two things – prosper us and make us successful. In order to receive that prosperity, we need divine revelation that we can only access through His help by incorporating the study of the Word of God into our daily routine. In Joshua 1.8, Moses counsels Joshua to do exactly that: "This book of the law shall not depart out of thy mouth; but thou shalt meditate therein day and night, that thou mayest observe to do according to all that is written therein: for then thou shalt make thy way prosperous, and then thou shalt have good success."

Incorporating the Word of God into our lives has many benefits. Among them are prosperity, good success, guidance, illumination, and understanding, especially when we have lost our way, wisdom, revelation, strength when we are weak, peace in troubled times, hope in times of despair, deliverance from evil, victory over our enemies, health, healing, long life, clarity in times of confusion, encouragement when we are discouraged, comfort and joy in times of sorrow, and the ability to live a pure life. The Divine Coach perfects and completes us.

Meditation on the Word leads to obedience, and obedience to the Word of God keeps you from falling into temptation. Here is what Solomon, in his wisdom, came to experience. In Proverbs 6:23-24, NASB, he writes, "For the commandment is a lamp and the teaching is light; and reproofs for discipline are the way of life, to keep you from the evil woman, from the smooth tongue of the adulteress." Similarly, the Word empowered David to live a pure life. In Psalm 119:9, he affirms, "How can a young person stay on the path of purity? By living according to your Word." In essence, believers can always turn to the Word for strength in times of temptation.

The Word of God is effective, certain, and infallible. It gives assurance and hope in times of despair. Isaiah 55:10-11 AMP states, "For as the rain and snow come down from the heavens, and return not there again, but water the earth and make it bring forth and sprout, that it may give seed to the sower and bread to the eater, so shall My word be that goes forth out of My mouth: it shall not return to Me void [without producing any effect, useless], but it shall accomplish that which I please and purpose, and it shall prosper in the thing for which I sent it."

Prayer, fasting and studying the Word of God are the foundational principles on which believers can establish and strengthen their relationship with God. Through intentional living, believers who want to experience the abundant life that Christ came to give us will seek the guidance and help of the Divine Coach.Only through prayer, fasting, and studying the Word of God will believers come to know who they are in Christ, be empowered to expand the Kingdom, enjoy the manifold blessings of being a child of God and understand what it means to be a Kingdom citizen. We are in the world, but we are not of this world. Thus the laws or principles we live by are not of this world. Instead, prayer, fasting, and studying the Word of God are the guiding principles that distinguish us as Kingdom citizens in this world. This practice is what allows us to respond appropriately to life's challenges. In the next chapter, I will share with you some appropriate and inappropriate responses to life challenges to clarify what I mean by being distinguished as a Kingdom citizen in this world.

CHAPTER IX

Appropriate Versus Inappropriate
Responses to Life's Challenges

Living life from the inside out is to experience the abundant,
fulfilled, satisfied, and successful life of significance.

Life challenges and adversities are common to everyone. What is not
common is the way we address them as you will hear from these
experiences I present in this chapter. When life challenges and adversities
shore up in your life you cannot ignore them. You have two choices. You can
either respond appropriately or you can choose to respond inappropriately.
However, now that you know of the intervening role of the Holy Spirit in
your life and now that you know how to access His help, you can choose
to seek His help and respond appropriately in faith or you can choose to
ignore His help and react inappropriately in fear. To react in fear is a clear
indication that you have not sought His Divine Counsel or you have not
obeyed His counsel. To respond in faith indicates that you have sought and
have chosen to follow His Divine counsel.

My Inappropriate Fear Response:

Life challenges and adversities are not foreign to me. I was and still am familiar with challenges and adversities in many domains of my life, especially in the financial, relational, geographical relocation and career life transition domains. And when they came my way, I initially did not always respond in faith because of my spiritual immaturity."

I began to experience financial challenges very early in life as poverty was all around me while growing up. However, had it not been for my grandmother's loving care and resilient faith, who raised me, shielded, and empowered me with her godly wisdom to respond to them, life challenges could have left me bitter instead of a better human being.

I grew up in a small village on a very tiny island in the Caribbean with such humble means and limited financial resources that I was the least likely to succeed in any area of my life. My mother left me in the care of my grandmother, who only had a first-grade education, but thankfully she was able to read and write. Her experience as a girl growing up with her mother and the kind of issues that young girls were still faced with when I was a teenager in her care contributed to her determination for me not to have the same experience she had when she was growing up.

My grandmother grew up in poverty stricken conditions. Her mother did not have the means to educate her or any of her siblings, which resulted in her growing up too fast, having to take care of her own needs and that of six children without the help of a spouse. My mother was the fourth of six children, and I was told that she was not only beautiful, she was also industrious, creative, hardworking, and loved by everyone in the village. Unfortunately, she followed in the footsteps of my grandmother. She became pregnant with me at the tender age of eighteen, and like her mother, she was also a single mother. In fact, it was a pervasive pattern. Most of the young girls around her age were getting pregnant out of wedlock, and that pattern didn't change when I came along.

To exacerbate the problem, the fathers were not marrying the women, nor were they taking financial responsibility for raising their children.

Therefore, women were either raising the children alone, or having multiple children to get help from another relationship, or the grandparents were charged with raising them. Those who could travel left their children with grandparents and older siblings and migrated to other Caribbean Islands seeking a better quality of life. Girls who were fortunate enough to grow up in wealthy families migrated to attend high school and universities on the larger Caribbean Islands. Since we were British citizens, colonized by England, many of the affluent boys and girls migrated to England while others went to North America and Canada to pursue careers in law, secretarial studies, and the health field.

The pervasive challenge teenage girls in my village faced was teenage pregnancy resulting in single parenthood. That was the norm when I was growing up. If any of the young girls were fortunate enough to get married, not only did they give birth to many children, my opinion is that most of them seemed unhappy and unfulfilled. From my observation, they lived in abject poverty in poor environments. There was no running water and sanitation was either non-existent or, at best, horrible.

From those who came to seek help in the form of credit from my grandmother, who had a convenience store, I heard that there was never enough money to feed or clothe these children, let alone send them to school. Many of these women looked trapped in these situations. At times, I heard stories of and even witnessed them being physically abused by partners or by their husbands if they were unfortunate enough to be married.

My grandmother escaped those abuses because, as she told me, she had a choice, and chose not to enter into marriage with any of her children's fathers because she had a vision for her life that did not include abuse. So, when my mother gave birth to me outside of wedlock, my grandmother did not see marriage to my father as a good resolution since my father was involved in another complicated relationship. According to her, she wanted my mother to be free to explore other and better options for her life. Thus, she encouraged her to leave home and go to Trinidad and Tobago to seek a better quality of life. It was the choice many other young women her age on our island exercised.

Mom followed my grandmother's advice and agreed to leave me in her care and went to live with her elder sister, who had migrated to Trinidad and Tobago with her husband and several children. The plan was that my mom would help care for her nieces and nephews until she could find more gainful employment. Thus, I was left in the loving care and guidance of my wise and godly grandmother until I graduated from high school and migrated to Grenada, where I started work at age 15. A year later, I got married to a Pastor who though much older than me, in my view was my best strategic response in the event my grandmother died. Having a husband meant that I would not be alone, and if my marriage did not work out, then I could always get divorced, since by this time with my educational level, I could earn enough to take care of myself. That was the strategy my grandmother gave me for a free and fulfilled life, and that was the perspective that I inherited. It was not mine; it was my grandmother's, the only authority figure I trusted in my life.

As previously mentioned, as a young girl, I didn't always respond to life challenges. In retrospect, because I was so young, I didn't know enough to respond. I thought I was responding in faith, but upon reflection, I was reacting in fear. Fear of poverty and fear of divorce led me to pursue and focus on getting an education.

In addition, the fear of losing my grandmother, who was always quite sickly while I was growing up, led me to get married at age 16. I reacted to the challenges of poverty, marital and spousal abuse in fear because I saw them through my grandmother's eyes and the authority figures in my life. The scriptures teach us that the things that we see are temporary. The things that we don't see are the things that are permanent. The old man's response to the challenges and adversities of the life events he encountered is instructive. At that time, I did not know that fear guided my initial reactions to the challenges I was observing in my environment and household. My mother had left, and my grandma was sick, and I didn't think she would live much longer. I felt I had no choice, and I had to have a strategy to respond to life challenges.

My grandmother's advice was, "Get an education and trust God to provide for you." Her words influenced me to focus on getting a high school education because I believed that it would be the pathway to a good quality of life, one that would give me the option to walk away from an abusive marriage. If I needed to, I would be able to take care of myself, but, let's face it, was I really trusting God and living by faith? Was this a life lived from the inside out, or was I reacting to the challenges around me in fear? I know now that I was not responding to my life challenges, I was reacting, and I was reacting in fear.

I was reacting in fear because I depended on my mental abilities and an education system that I trusted would deliver a well-paying job when I graduated. At that time, though, I was too young to be able to determine that. Perhaps if I were to ask my grandmother today, she would tell me that what she meant was that I should depend totally on God and the inner voice of wisdom, the Holy Spirit, our Divine Coach, and not lean on my own understanding. I know that now because as I grew older and life challenges continued to come my way, I had to develop an intimate relationship with God, and quite naturally when I turned my life over to God at the age of fifteen, I also received the gift of the baptism of the Holy Spirit. As I continued to develop a closer relationship with God, I became familiar with the voice of the Holy Spirit, my inner Guide, Helper, and Divine Coach.

This is the life I later came to describe as living inside out – a life of faith and total dependence on the leading of the Holy Spirit. Indeed, living by faith is living our lives from the inside out. The Holy Spirit allows us to see things that are permanent in the realm of the spirit. The scriptures confirm in 2 Corinthians 4:18 that the things we see in the natural world are not permanent, but the things we don't see in the spirit realm are the ones that are permanent or even eternal.

The scriptures also advise us that we should welcome adversity as friends. Obviously, to my natural eyes, poverty, psychological spousal abuse, and illiteracy were not my friends, so I did not welcome them. They were temporal, according to the scriptures, meant to make me a strong woman of faith, but, to my natural eyes, they were not temporary. I saw that they would be permanent if I did not have a strategy to confront them. I saw them as my enemies, not my friends. It was up to me to do something about them, or else they would consume me. I was terrified of what I was seeing around me. I had no relationship with the Holy Spirit at the time. I came to know him much later. I was a young Catholic girl at the time, and although I practiced prayer and all the sacraments of the church, I did not yet have the help of the Divine Coach; I did not have spiritual eyes. Therefore, I reacted instead of responding to life's challenges when they showed up.

Appropriate Responses To Life's Challenges and Adversities

Joseph's Response

We do not always take the time to pray and ask the Divine Coach for help or even reflect on life challenges and adversities when they shore up in our lives. If we did, I promise you that the outcome you receive would be totally different from the one I shared with you above.

The story of Joseph in Genesis (Chapters 37:3 – 50:26) and his attitude towards difficulty and misfortune highlights an appropriate response to life's challenges and adversities when they shore up in our lives. Joseph and his brother Benjamin were born to their father, Jacob, and his mother, Rachael, whom Jacob loved dearly in his old age. In fact, Rachael died while she was giving birth to Benjamin. As is the case in some families, Jacob showed extreme affection to the sons of the wife he loved. Jacob's affection for Joseph aroused the jealousy of his other brothers. Their jealousy was exacerbated when Joseph shared some very disturbing dreams with them in which he was portrayed as ruling over his brethren.

They were so incensed with Joseph that they began to look for any opportunity to get rid of him and kill Joseph. First, they threw him into a pit but eventually at the pleading of one of his brothers, sold him to some slave traders who took him to Egypt and sold him to Potiphar, one of King Pharaoh's ministers. The brothers never told Joseph's father what they did to Joseph, so Jacob assumed Joseph was dead.

Joseph encountered many challenges while he was serving in Egypt. He was a devoted believer in God, and though his brothers treated him so poorly, he maintained his relationship with God and served his master Potiphar loyally. This caused him to find favor in Potiphar's eyes; having observed that his household was blessed upon Joseph's arrival, he wisely entrusted all his household affairs into Joseph's hands. But this favor was short-lived. Potiphar's wife falsely accused him of sexually assaulting her and Joseph was imprisoned for several years. You would think that this would undermine Joseph's faith in God. This would be a natural reaction. But Joseph responded by maintaining his devotion to God. As a result, God allowed him to find favor with the warden and he was again promoted to a leadership position in the prison. He didn't refuse the position as you might have expected him to do. Instead, he responded by faithfully serving in his leadership position as well; this was another appropriate response. Finally, after twelve years of faithful service as the Warden assistant in prison, because of his devotion to God and his humility, God created an opportunity for Joseph to use his gift of interpretation of dreams to have him released from prison. First, in the prison he correctly interpreted the dreams of two prisoners and as a result, when the right time came God used him again to interpret a dream that the King of Egypt himself had and which no one but Joseph could interpret.

By this time, Joseph, then thirty, because of his correct interpretation of the Pharaoh's dreams where he divinely predicted that the world would experience seven years of abundance followed by seven years of famine, Joseph was again Pharaoh to a leadership position in Egypt, second only to the king himself who tasked him with preparing the nation for the years of famine joseph predicted would follow the years of abundance.

Note Joseph's response in each one of the situations he found himself. He had a choice to react or to respond. But he decided to respond by remaining faithful to God. He could have blamed God for all his misfortunes with his brothers and in Egypt. For Joseph these were not just challenges. These were life adversities. He had no control over how he was treated but he had control over his responses. He could have chosen not to interpret the dreams of the two prisoners. But, he did. He could have chosen not to interpret Pharaoh's dreams when they sent for him, but he did.

How could Joseph remain faithful to God when it seems as though God Himself turned his back on him? His resilient faith in God controlled his responses. Had he not responded in faith and with such grace and humility when faced with his adversities, his outcome could have been different. Consider what could have happened had he not trusted God and reacted in fear. Perhaps he may never have seen his father and his brothers again. He would not have had the opportunity to be ruler in Egypt and in that position, or had the opportunity to save the world from a dire famine. And perhaps he would have married, but who is to say whether he would have been blessed with a priestess for a spouse and have two wonderful sons who, as he said, caused him to forget all that he suffered at the hands of his brothers in Canaan.

Joseph's story highlights the appropriate response to life challenges and adversities. Life will always present us with all kinds of challenges, and on occasion, we can choose to respond by doing the right thing by waiting on God to deliver us, or we could choose to react by leaning on our own human understanding. He demonstrated the proper attitude towards the difficulties and misfortunes he suffered at the hands of his brothers and Potiphar's wife. Joseph responded in faith instead of reacting in fear because he had a different perspective concerning all that happened to him. Read his perspective as he shared it with his brothers:

> *"And now do not be distressed, or angry with yourselves, because you sold me here; for God sent me before you to preserve life. For the famine has been in the land these two years; and*

there are yet five years in which there will be neither plowing nor harvest. And God sent me before you to preserve for you a remnant on earth, and to keep alive."

(Genesis 45:5-7 RSV; NIV)

Joseph recognized that God ordained all the travails he had undergone to ensure the survival of Egypt and the surrounding countries. Knowing that God is always faithful to His promise, Joseph was able to forgive his brothers' animosity towards him instead of reacting by giving them exactly what they deserved. Though he did not know how life would turn out when he was sold into slavery, his resilient faith in God informed his perspective and kept him from compromising when faced with life's challenges.

Mary's Response

Mary, a dear friend of mine, shared the following story of the mysterious death of her twenty-five-year-old son in a book entitled, *Brokenhearted: A Mother's Journey to Wholeness*. This painful story illustrates how the power of the Divine Coach, combined with the practical application of her resilient faith, empowers us to respond in faith rather than react in fear when faced with life's challenges and adversities.

> *"We arrived at his school apartment to find that he had departed, not for school or home but from earth to heaven, from mortality to immortality. In a state of shock, my soul was separated from my body like an out-of-body experience. I was staring at myself in total disbelief as if I were watching a movie where this woman lost her only son. I carried on conversations with the police, who were asking questions only a mother would know. I proceeded to identify birthmarks and give height, weight, and size without internalizing the fact*

that my promised son, had indeed departed without saying goodbye."[6]

Mary described how immensely calm she was while watching, listening, and going over details and plans with her husband about notifying family members and how to shelter their two girls from the shock of losing their only brother. She continued in *"a state of suspended reality, shock denial and emotional emptiness for many days."*[7] In fact, throughout the entire ordeal and weeks after the traumatic incident, Maria explained that she experienced an unusual calm that could only come from the comforting presence of the Holy Spirit.

"Although I was calm, yet I was very uncomfortable and restless. I found myself sitting in many places, inside the car one minute, outside on the pavement another minute. I paced back and forth endlessly, still in total disbelief and denial. The police had instructed that we could not enter his apartment. I complied without any struggle or defiance. I obeyed the police instructions, which I normally would do; but, when it comes to my children, that is another matter. My son called me Mama Goose because he said that I tended to hover over my children, always so protective of them. Yet, in that moment of desperation, shock and disbelief overwhelmed me to the point that I could not protest or defy the police's instruction and fight my way into the apartment to see who was in there. I was convinced that whoever was inside the apartment had nothing, absolutely nothing to do with my son. I did not cry; in an altered reality, it was a movie playing with my soul suspended from my body.

A body bag was rolled out of the house on a stretcher to be transported to the mortuary. The police who stayed behind to debrief my husband and I said, "there will be an investigation as there was no forced entry, but whoever he opened the door to and allowed inside his home was no stranger to him." We left for home, an hour and thirty minutes' drive that

---

[6] Mary I. Edosomwan, D. Min, *Broken Hearted: A Mother's Journey to Wholeness* (Mary I. Edosomwan,DMin, 2020)

[7] Ibid

seemed like a life journey. The state of suspended reality, shock, and denial continued. I felt emotionally empty, dead on the inside. I was in a zombie state or numbness, as described by (Kubler Ross) for many days.

My girls came home as well as other family members. I was the one consoling everybody. I remember hearing people say how strong I was in carrying on a conversation as though my son was still alive. To me, he was still alive. As family members departed to their respective homes, cities, and states in the days following the burial, my heart broke. I could feel the blood flowing from my heart into my stomach in total disbelief. Suddenly, I am awakened to the reality of my loss as the connection between body and mind is reunited. I remember saying to myself repeatedly, "So it is true? My son is gone?" Grief like an avalanche rapidly overtook my mind and overwhelmed my spirit, and its weight broke my body as I collapsed to the floor with uncontrollable tears. My heart was broken and shattered into too many pieces, but for those who believe in the saving grace of God, King Jesus is the only one who can put your broken pieces together again."[8]

God, the Holy Spirit, her Divine Comforter, and Healer had initiated Mary's journey from brokenness and sorrow to wholeness through various stages of grief which she described in her book. In that book, Mary describes her journey. She credits the Holy Spirit with the inner strength she was endowed with as she went through that painful journey from broken heartedness to wholeness. In her testimony, she shares how the Holy Spirit worked in her to help her to respond to this painful life adversity by giving her the power to forgive whoever her son's killer was. The natural human reaction would have been to demand vengeance, but she responded in faith, leaving it up to God to let His Divine will be done. In Mary's words, "It took six years of reconstruction for me to find complete healing." According to her, "This healing was only made possible by the God who specializes in doing the impossible."

The Holy Spirit is the spirit of revelation, and Mary's relationship with the Divine Coach is the secret to that amazing response. She would never

---

[8] Ibid

have been able to respond with such resilient faith had the Divine Coach not revealed Himself to her in the entire process of her healing. The Holy Spirit works in an amazing way in the life of believers to ever prepare them for life's challenges and adversities. The Holy Spirit had revealed to Mary that her son was going to die prior to his death. She said she prayed and fasted for 21 days for God's intervention, but according to her, "the unthinkable still happened."

Several times during her grief, Mary would ask the question, "why would God allow such a thing to happen to me? But, she said, "the question was not part of her lament. God was gracious to forewarn me, and He loved me enough to show me the misery ahead." She remembered how "the Holy Spirit empowered me to worship God in the midst of the challenge of pain, suffering, and the shame of feeling less than a mother." She couldn't understand how in her role as a Minister when she prayed to God to spare the lives of other children, He would answer her prayers, but when she prayed for God to spare the life of her own son, He did not grant her request. That she said was very painful for her to bear.

Revelation is one of the amazing benefits Christians receive from the Holy Spirit. Through the Holy Spirit, God reveals His purposes and plans to believers. 2 Corinthians 2:9-10 confirms, "But as it is written, eye hath not seen, nor ear heard, neither have entered into the heart of man, the things which God hath prepared for them that love him. But God hath revealed them unto us by His Spirit: for the Spirit searcheth all things, yea, the deep things of God."

Like in the case of Joseph, the Holy Spirit revealed Himself to Mary and taught her many valuable lessons in the midst of her pain and suffering and during the process of her healing. He taught her that God only allows those He could trust to have painful life challenges. In fact, she said that He revealed to her that it was a privilege to experience challenges and adversities in life because they are meant for our spiritual development. This is how she reflected those sentiments in her book.

"The privilege of losing a child or children yet refusing to curse God is uncommon among the human population. Blessed are you that God will count you faithful enough to try you, to feel the unbearable, inhumane, and ungodly painful emotions of losing a child. Similarly, God gave His only begotten Son to die a cruel death on the cross for you and I as an act of love. Can those chosen to follow in God's footsteps love Him enough to experience the pain of loss without cursing God? Grief, by any other name, is pain; and God almighty knows all about your heartache and the agony of your loss."[9]

Although Mary's life experiences and Joseph's were different, their responses to life's challenges and adversities were similar. I would even dare to say that they share the same perception as that of the old man at the beginning of my book. They both saw their adversity as God-ordained; therefore, they responded by trusting in God's love and thus in His divine intervention. According to them, God in His divine wisdom allows life challenges and adversities to fulfill His divine purposes. To Mary, God allowed her son's death "so other grief sufferers would have a road map to achieving wholeness." To Joseph, his suffering at the hands of his brothers was allowed to save many lives in a worldwide famine. These lived experiences confirm the Scripture in Jeremiah 29:11-13 and Romans 8:28 that God indeed has a plan for your life.

"For I know the plans I have for you, declares the Lord, plans for good and not for evil, to give you a future and a hope. Then you will call upon me, come and pray to me, and I will hear you. You will seek me and find me when you seek me with all your heart."

(Jeremiah 29:11-13 ESV)

---

[9] Ibid

"And we know that all things work together for good to those who love God, to those who are called according to His purpose."

(Romans 8:28 KJV)

Mary sought the Lord's direction, and through the Divine Coach, God guided her into the unfinished (graduate) school program left undone by her son's untimely death. She later recalled in her book where she described her experience: "I completed it without knowing what God was going to do for me and through me. In the process of putting the pieces of my broken heart together, He birthed a process that will heal and mend broken hearts among Christians and unbelievers across the world; but first, He had to do the same thing for me."

The police have not yet found who killed Mary's son and I asked her how she felt about that. As she recounted the story with tears in her eyes, she told me, "God knows who did it. I am going to leave it in the hands of God." Her friends encouraged her to continue with the case to find his killer and have that person prosecuted and brought to justice so she could get closure. But, she told me, "As a woman of God who has received God's forgiveness, I have been able to let go of revenge, forgive, and move on with my life." I asked her what, in her opinion, was responsible for her resilience, her resolve, and her ability to forgive his killer. She quietly responded, and with admirable conviction, "The Holy Spirit strengthened and is continuing to strengthen me."

Mary is not afraid to forgive because she enjoys God's perfect love, which is one of the gifts of the Holy Spirit, our Divine Coach. God's perfect love casts out all fear and allows us to exercise self-control. We are able to control our emotions despite the pain and grief that adversity brings. I don't want you to think that forgiving and exercising self-control are easy. They come only through the empowering presence of the Divine Coach.

My friend has been able to turn that pain into power. Now, she memorializes the loss of her son each year in the form of an annual grief conference where she brings together family members and people of faith who experienced grief so that they can celebrate the life of their loved ones.

When life challenges and adversities come your way, no matter how difficult and heartbreaking they may be, the important thing to remember is that the experience is for a divine purpose. Like Mary, when you respond to life challenges in faith by obeying the voice of the Divine Coach instead of reacting in fear, the outcome will not only make you into a better version of yourself, it will bring great glory to God.

An Inappropriate Reaction: Auntie Leanna's Reaction

After being married to her husband, Herbert, for several years, Auntie Leanna became very ill. She was physically unable to walk and was relegated to a wheelchair for the rest of her life, and since they had no children, her husband, Uncle Herbert had to take care of her. He cooked, cleaned, washed, shopped, and attended to all of her physical needs as well. Uncle Herbert was a commercial fisherman who was very generous; I think he gave away as much fish as he sold. He was also a soft-spoken, kind, patient, and godly man. These character traits were demonstrated in the way he cared for his wife and the contribution he made to the well-being of the people in the village he lived in. This is the environment Uncle Herbert created for himself and his wife. Though Auntie Leanna was physically challenged, she seemed very happy; in fact, they both seemed very happy, and he took excellent care of her. He never complained, at least I never heard him complain, and most importantly, she never complained. They lived together in these circumstances for over thirty years. Given how healthy Uncle Herbert was and how sick Auntie Leanna had been, naturally, we all expected Uncle Herbert would outlive Auntie Leanna. Still, one day, out of the blue, without being sick, Uncle Herbert died.

The death of Uncle Herbert left her bitter. After his death, Auntie Leanna missed her husband so terribly that she started to complain. She literally became so angry with God that I would say she cursed the God she had believed in. She blamed God for his death and became depressed and was quite miserable. Her complaints did not help, and she became sicker and sicker.

Many family members took responsibility for looking after her when Uncle Herbert died. Someone was hired to take care of her as she could not do anything for herself. Her niece was married to my uncle, so I visited her regularly and did whatever I could to make her comfortable. I continued to visit her even after I married, left home, and migrated to another country. Auntie Leanna felt that God had abandoned her. Because we were both of the Christian faith, I tried to encourage her in the word of God. My intent was to help her to see how good God still was to her. He had not abandoned her. She still had us. We were there to take care of her though God took Uncle Herbert from her, as she continually said. She did not want me to talk to her about the goodness of God and his faithfulness. One day, when I was visiting her, she screamed at me and said that God could not love her as I was telling her. What kind of God would show love by taking away the only person she had in life who loved her? She could not understand that. Although I assured her that we loved her and would continue to take care of her, which by the way I told her how God was showing love to her, she would have none of that talk.

Auntie Leanna wanted to die, but she lived for many years. When she did die, she died angry, bitter, afraid, and unforgiving. To my knowledge, she never forgave God for taking from her the one person she loved and who loved her in life. After reading Auntie Leanna's story, you might ask yourself, why were Joseph and my friend Mary able to respond to life challenges so differently. Mary and Joseph were able to forgive those who wronged them, while Auntie Leanna was not. Life will always present us with a series of challenges that will test our faith, character, and resilience. If viewed as opportunities, we can respond by leveraging them to become the best version of ourselves. Our perspective of those challenges will determine whether we respond or react. Because of their perspective and faith in God, Joseph and Mary responded by forgiving. Auntie Leanna had the same choice, and she chose not to forgive God; she reacted in fear. Joseph and Mary's faith-based responses are what I would call appropriate responses. However, I would classify Auntie Leanna's fear-based response as an inappropriate one. In the next section, I will discuss the differences between both.

Fear-Based Versus Faith-Based Responses

There is a distinct difference between fear-based and faith-based responses. A fear-based response is outside-in living, and faith-based living is inside-out living. The person who reacts to life challenges and adversities in fear lives life from the outside in. That person either relies on the voices and noises in the external environment which inform their conscious mind or from his/her own belief system in the subconscious mind. These external and internal environmental noises and self-limiting beliefs may come from their socioeconomic background, cultural or racial-ethnic background, and political affiliations. Such a person forfeits the internal wisdom and guidance of the Divine Coach freely available to them. However, the person who responds by faith is the one who lives life from the inside out and depends on the internal voice of unlimited divine guidance, wisdom, knowledge, and understanding, that is, the voice of the Holy Spirit, the Divine Coach within.

Fear-Based Living Outcome and Consequences

Fear-based living reacts to life challenges and adversities by relying on voices and noises in the external environment. The experiences of the Israelites in the wilderness on their way to the Promised Land are a good example of fear-based living and the consequences. For four hundred and thirty years, the children of Israel, descendants of Abraham, Isaac, and Jacob, lived in slavery in Egypt. Then, when they could bear it no more, they cried out to God in faith, obviously inherited from their forefather Abraham, for deliverance. Four hundred and thirty years before, God revealed to Abraham that his descendants would be enslaved in a foreign land but promised them that He would deliver them. Sure enough, when they cried out to God, at the appointed time, God sent Moses to deliver them from Egypt as He promised, and they were to settle in the land of Canaan, which today we know as Israel. That was the promise of God, and it was specific. They were to go back to the Promised Land, and no one would be able to uproot them from there.

However, the many challenges on the way to the Promised Land caused the Israelites to fear. First, they encountered the challenge of escaping the Egyptian army at the bank of the Red Sea. They had only two choices the way they saw it. It was either surrender to Pharaoh or fight Pharaoh's large army. Crossing the Red Sea was not an option, or so they thought. However, Moses's faith in God's Word to deliver them prevailed over Pharaoh's army, and Israel stepped onto the highway that God created in the midst of the sea, something that they could have only experienced by faith and crossed over on dry land to the other side while Pharaoh's army drowned in the sea. Their faith in God resulted in their deliverance from slavery.

The Red Sea was not the only challenge the Israelites faced on their journey to the Promised Land. Soon, Israel faced thirst and hunger in the desert. With scorching heat and cold desert nights, the Israelites forgot the God who miraculously delivered them from four hundred and thirty years of slavery in Egypt with amazing signs and wonders. They forgot how He miraculously parted the Red Sea and delivered them from their slave masters. Thirst and hunger, heat and cold, lack of water, and parched dry land caused them to be fearful.

Instead of turning to God in faith, they gave in to their fear and threatened to kill Moses and raise up a leader to take them back to slavery in Egypt. In their view, it was better to be enslaved in Egypt than to die a slow and painful death of hunger and thirst in the desert. This display of doubt and insecurity resulted in them never entering the promised land; they got exactly what they desired.

God was so displeased with their lack of faith in His promise that although He gave them water to drink and angel food to eat, that generation that left Egypt, including Moses and Aaron, their chosen leaders, died in the desert. They died in the desert because of their double-mindedness.

Only Joshua and Caleb entered the Promised Land because they trusted God, despite their challenges.

When Christians fear, it is a sign of double-mindedness. It shows a lack of trust in the delivering power of the Holy Spirit, our Divine Coach, to help us when we face life's challenges.God says He did not give us a spirit of fear but of power, of love, a calm and well-balanced mind, discipline and self-control. When we are afraid, our minds are not well-balanced, as God describes. When we fear or doubt God, we are said to be double-minded (James 1:8). The Apostle James says that when a person comes to God, he must do so in faith:

> "Only *it must be in faith that he asks with no wavering (no hesitating, no doubting)…For truly, let not such a person imagine that he will receive anything [he asks for] from the Lord, [For being as he is] a man of two minds (hesitating, dubious, irresolute), [he is] unstable and unreliable and uncertain about everything [he thinks, feels, decides]"*
>
> (James 1:6-8 AMPC).

That is exactly what Satan wants to do to you with the Spirit of fear. He wants to make you unstable, unreliable, and uncertain about everything: your thoughts, God's promises. Anyone who has ever been afraid can attest to the truth of that scripture.

This is what fear-based living did to me when I prematurely married at such a young age. I didn't trust God to take care of me if my grandmother died before I was old enough and mature enough to marry. My action was one of double-mindedness. I trusted God and trusted my husband's protection at the same time. However, years later, as a consequence of fear, doubt, and insecurity, the marriage did not turn out the way I expected, and we eventually divorced. I had to learn to trust the direction of the Holy Spirit.Those relationship challenges taught me not to be double-minded, unstable, and uncertain. Instead, I learned how to develop a partnership with the Divine Coach. In that partnership, I learned to by faith as the

Bible admonishes us to do. The Holy Spirit taught me how to faith my fears to death!

Several years later, when the pain and disappointment I experienced in my first marriage subsided, I married a second time. I was now older and wiser, or so I thought. I knew what I wanted out of a relationship, and this time I did not want a Christian, nor did I want to marry a Pastor. The first marriage and my experiences with the church members etched in my brain that they could not be trusted. I wanted an educated man who loved me and had the economic means to provide for my son and me. This man also had to be well respected in society, and I should be proud of him. But, most importantly, he should respect me. Thankfully, in my view, I found just the person that I wanted. He was educated, smart, well-respected in society and he provided a wonderful home for my son and me. I had made a good life decision. In fact, you could say that marrying him moved me into the upper-middle class, something I might not have been able to accomplish that quickly on my own. We later moved to Central America as diplomats. This is where my son had the privilege to be educated in one of the top schools in the country and where I had the opportunity to go to college and obtain a bachelor's degree.

Life was great until it wasn't. Infidelity again, like cancer, attacked my second marriage. After the first marriage ended in divorce, I had vowed that I would never be part of organized religion anymore, so I stopped going to church altogether and intentionally stopped socializing with other Christians. Needless to say, when infidelity entered my second marriage, I was not able to hear the voice of the Divine Coach as I used to when I had a healthy prayer life and was in an environment with other believers. I began to fear once again not only for my marriage but for my son. When he was born, I had promised the Lord that I would raise him in the Christian faith. I had a change of heart occasioned by the pain I experienced with his biological father, a pastor. I vowed then that there was nothing of that Christian lifestyle I wanted, so I reacted to that life challenge I was facing, and I married a non-believer; I became unequally yoked.

I should tell you that although my second husband had all the earthly qualities I was seeking in a partner, he lacked the most important thing, which, at the time, I didn't think was so important. He did not have a relationship with God. So, how could he love me the way Christ instructed husbands to love their wives as their own flesh? He couldn't because He didn't know Christ, nor did he know the Divine Coach. The scriptures tell us that the world cannot receive the Divine Coach. He is the gift of God only to believers. Needless to say, being unequally yoked in the Spirit was the first ingredient for another failed marriage. Problems began long before we married and moved to Barbados and Central America. I was too busy reacting to all the relationship challenges I was facing at that time in my life.

My perception of the members and leaders in the Body of Christ was that they were all abusive and that I didn't need to be in that environment. I didn't want anything to do with organized religion, and I said that I would never marry a man of God. Well, I began reaping just what I sowed. Life and death, the Scriptures tell us, are in the power of the tongue. I had sown the wind and was reaping the whirlwind. Naturally, without the direction of the Divine Coach, the Body of Christ, prayer, fasting, the wisdom of good godly Christian leadership to guide me, and the word of God, I was reacting to life challenges. I was not responding. My marriage had become too unbearable, and that was definitely not the life I wanted. I resorted to what I knew best; I resorted to prayer.

Faith-based Living, Outcome, and Consequences

One day, when the pain of loneliness and emotional abuse in my marriage became so overwhelming, in a moment of desperation, I again started crying out to God to deliver me. I remember that day clearly. I was about to go into my room again to pray when I clearly heard the voice of the Divine Coach in the depth of my being, encouraging me to return to the household of faith to join myself with other believers. He said, "It is time for you to go back to church. It is time to join yourself again with my people who love me. That's where you belong."

Later that week, He also reminded me of earlier promises I had made to Him to raise my son as a believer in Christ and pass on my faith to him. In addition, I had promised two years prior that if He delivered me completely from the life of infidelity I had found myself in, I would dedicate the rest of my life entirely to Him. He reminded me that the fact I was now living in Central America was proof that He had made good on that deliverance. Now, it was my turn to make good on my promises.

That was a defining moment in my life. In response to the voice of the Divine Coach that day, I immediately started looking for a church to be a part of. I thought it would not be easy to find a church where I could fellowship because I had recently moved to Costa Rica and didn't speak Spanish so well. I needed to find an English-speaking church where my son and I could fellowship, and I did.

I recalled that one of my colleagues where I taught English as a second language had extended an open invitation to join her at her church, where the services were conducted in English. That day I telephoned her, and the following Sunday, Yvonne came to my home and took me to her church. I was grateful that God had already gone ahead of me and prepared not only the church where I could fellowship, He also prepared the right person to introduce me to that body of believers.

As I entered the service on the first Sunday, I knew that God had led me there because the worship, the word, the love of the believers were more than I could ask for. To confirm, He gave me Yvonne, a wonderful woman of God who later became my dearest friend and spiritual mentor. God used her mightily in my life, and my relationship with Christ grew by leaps and bounds. Yvonne introduced me to home Bible study fellowships, where I deepened my relationship with Jesus Christ. He would later use her during our mentorship relationship to encourage me to respond to the call of God in my life to enroll in a Bible College. In the Bible College in Central America, I was introduced to life in the Spirit. A little while after, I received the Baptism of the Holy Spirit with the evidence of speaking in an unknown tongue. This was something that I doubted was authentic for many years.

God not only proved to me that the Baptism of the Holy Spirit was authentic, He so radically changed my life that from that day to now, my life has never been the same again. As my relationship with God deepened, the infidelity in my marriage, which had started several years prior to moving to Central America, worsened, and my relationship with my second husband grew worse. The marriage was so riddled with insensitivity and emotional abuse that my second marriage ended in divorce after sixteen years of enduring emotional pain.

I realize now, in both the first and second marriage, I was still double-minded. I was trusting God on the one hand, and on the other, I was leaning on my own understanding. Early in my life, when marital challenges came, instead of responding by depending on the guidance of the Divine Coach, I listened to the voices of past authority figures, background socialization, and the experiences internalized from the environment in which I was surrounded and reacted in fear by resorting to having a divorce.

Life Outcomes and Consequences Resulting From Responding in Faith Versus Reacting In Fear

Faith-based living is a developmental process; it is not automatic. In the process, the continued challenges you encounter in life could make you bitter or better. The challenges and adversities I experienced in my first two marriages and the death of my first grandchild at age 11 months played a pivotal role in strengthening my faith and developing an intimate relationship with God. I learned to rely on the voice of the Holy Spirit, my Divine Coach, when several years later, in 2008, after sixteen years of marriage, my third husband lost his life in a fatal car accident in Tanzania.

I've had relationship challenges that plagued my life from early childhood; I simply could not seem to escape them. It seems that I am doomed to what I would call unavailable love. My definition of unavailable love is my inability to find a life partner who is emotionally available for me.

You see, for twenty-one years, my life had gone through several transitions relationally and geographically. I married twice and moved five times. If you recall, when I first got married at the tender age of sixteen, it was because of fear. My grandmother was old and constantly getting sick. I was afraid she would die, and I would be left all alone in the world to fend for myself. Though she raised me to trust in God, I married twice out of fear. The first time I needed a companion and friend. The second time I needed a father for my son and a husband to provide for me the quality of life, I feared that I could not have alone. However, after two failed marriages, my grandmother was still alive, so I feared in vain; I did not trust God at all.

With that fate of unavailable love looming large over my head, I moved to the United States, bent on living a single life dedicated to God forever. My son no longer needed a dad; in fact, looking back, neither of them really provided him with the paternal guidance I had expected. I practically raised him alone with the help and guidance of the Holy Spirit, and I am so glad I did. He migrated to Canada, and I migrated to the United States.

Bruised, battered, and tired from the emotional pain I suffered from my first two marriages, I was still bent on remaining single and serving God. Still, one day, I again felt the pain of loneliness, and I cried out to God to restore my relationship with my second husband. When I moved, I was not yet divorced, and I continued to seek the Lord in prayer with fasting and tears. My son had joined me in the United States by this time, so I was not experiencing as much loneliness as before. However, I still could not shake off the feeling of loneliness. It is amazing how when God wants to do something in your life. He will put the desire in your heart, have you cry out to Him, and then give you the desire of His heart for you while making you think it was your desire in the first place. So, I continued to cry out to God for the restoration of my marriage. But, all the while, I was getting reports that my husband was deeply involved in another relationship.

One night, while in prayer, I heard myself telling the Lord how unhappy I was and how lonely I was. I admitted to Him that I was truly not happy in my current marriage and asked Him to change my husband's heart and give him a heart for me. A heart that accepted me and loved me for who

I was and not who he wanted me to be. I actually reminded Him that He was the heart surgeon of all heart surgeons, and changing the heart of my husband should not be too hard for Him. After all, He created hearts. However, God did not answer that prayer. Instead, He brought me another heart that was capable of loving me for who I was. He gave me a husband who was the type of man I had been seeking for all these years, a man who knew the value and purpose of a wife.

A year after migrating to the United States, I met my third husband on the job, it was a divine connection; I knew it from the onset. He had migrated to the United States on assignment to the department that I was heading, and my heart loved him at first sight. I later learned that he had the same experience. Three years after seeking God in prayer and fasting for confirmation to be sure that He was the man I should trust with my tender heart that was broken so many times, we got married. We had sixteen years of happiness and fulfillment.

What was different? I had learned to trust God. I had learned that I did not need a husband to complete me. I was complete in God. I had come into the marriage not broken but whole. God had healed my heart, and I was now a complete woman of God who could love without unrealistic expectations of my spouse. I knew he was not perfect, and I didn't expect perfection. I depended on the Holy Spirit to help us through the initial challenging years because there were some challenges, but I was not afraid this time. I trusted God and the wisdom of the word of God to guide us through.

The Holy Spirit was the voice of wisdom and reason in my heart, and when I followed that voice of wisdom, I responded to life challenges instead of reacting. For example, we always forgave each other immediately when we made mistakes. We would never let the sun go down on our issues. We resolved them in love. In the past, I was looking for a way out because of fear of being hurt. Now, I was not afraid of being hurt, I could be hurt and yet forgive. So I was prepared to be hurt and to forgive.

The Scriptures teach us that perfect love casts out all fear, but this love was not human love; it is the perfect love of God. I was confident in God's perfect love so I could accept the imperfect love of another human being, which was made perfect by the love of Christ and the power of the Holy Spirit in my heart. God had healed me and prepared me for the tragedy that I was to experience on March 6, 2008.

Responding To Life Challenges Made Me Better Not Bitter

On that day, at 11:30 am, I heard a knock on my front door. I did not expect anyone, but my son, who had previous knowledge of the visitors and why they were coming, let them in the house. They came to bring me the devastating news that my husband, who had worked with an international development organization to ensure that orphans and vulnerable children in Africa had a better quality of life, had lost his life in a tragic car accident in Tanzania, Africa. As he was used to doing for sixteen years, he had gone to Africa to work on a Social Assistance Fund Project which he managed for the international organization that employed him. He gave his life working with the people he loved: widows, orphans, and vulnerable children in Africa.

This was the most painful news I had ever received in life. At that moment, I knew that if I gave in to the pain I was experiencing, I could quite possibly die from grief. I am a woman of great faith with the conviction that everything that happened to me in this life was directed by God. I had developed an intimate relationship with God in prayer over the years. I brought every life experience, whether good or bad, to God in prayer, and this is what I did at that time. I immediately went to my prayer closet, a special place in my home that I have dedicated to praying.

There, I prayed for God to strengthen me and help me. I remember that I articulated there on my knees how good God had been to me over the years. I didn't ask God why He did that to me, why He took my husband from me, or how could He allow that to happen to me? Instead, I remember committing the rest of my life in God's hands to care for me. There on my knees, I affirmed the words of Job, who went through great physical and mental adversity: "Though you slay me," and, I added, ``I know you won't slay me, "I will continue to put my trust in you."

I trust you must have heard from my experience that developing resilience cannot be done in isolation. In order to develop resilience, you will need to surround yourself with other resilient people, people who have similar perspectives on life challenges and adversities, and who will encourage you to grow from the changes and transitions you are experiencing.

Now, I know that every one of us has faced some type of life challenge or adversity. Each one of us has experienced some type of life change and has gone through some type of transition in our life. Each of us, for example, has transitioned from childhood into a teenager and from a teenager into adulthood. Some of you have had to transition from being single to married. Most of us have transitioned from being a student to an employee or from being a student to an entrepreneur or a business leader. Some of you have transitioned from living with and parenting kids to returning to what is described as an empty nest when all the kids have left home. What about transitioning from being married to becoming single again, either because of the death of a spouse or a divorce.

Some of you have lost jobs and had to deal with unemployment or have suffered the loss of someone dear to you, a parent, a child, or a grandchild. Some of you have experienced the loss of all or most of your life savings or investments. For some of you, either your parents, spouse or you may have made career changes and moved from one geographical location to another. The list of changes, challenges, adversities, and transitions could go on and on.

So, life brings each one of us changes, challenges, and adversities, and with each change, we find ourselves in a season of transition. You see, the one constant we have in life is change itself, and while most of us tend to want to resist change, it is difficult to resist change. So, what you and I must do is not to resist change but to engage in change and learn from it, so we become the best version of ourselves.

So what do you do when life shows up? Do you respond, or do you react to life challenges, and are you able to observe how you transition and transform as a result of the adversities, challenges, and changes life brings you? These are the questions I would like you to reflect on.

As we respond to the challenges and changes which COVID-19, for example, has brought to the globe, would you respond in faith by tuning in to your internal environment and listening to the Divine Coach, or would you react in fear by listening to the many voices, like the news media, and the political and religious authority figures in your external environment? If you want to experience abundant living, you can choose to go within.

In this world, you and I will be faced with diverse challenges, but we must not be surprised when we do as according to 1 Peter 4:12: "Dear friends, do not be surprised at the fiery ordeal that has come on you to test you, as though something strange was happening to you." The level of thinking you bring to the challenge will depend on whether you respond or react to life challenges. In other words, your mindset and your belief system will determine your choice to respond or react, fight or flight, embrace and leverage or resist.

There is a process that leads up to the response or reaction to your decision to embrace or resist. First comes your perception of the challenge, which is controlled by your belief system or your mindset. Then comes your response or your reaction. Depending on your perception or your mindset, you will either respond or react. If you view the challenge as an opportunity for growth, you will embrace the challenge and work through it until you accomplish the desired outcome. Working through them means that you are leveraging them to your advantage to achieve the desired outcome resulting in you becoming stronger and even more resilient. If you see the challenge as something meant to harm you, then fear takes over, and the outcome would not be what you desire; in fact, it could be disastrous.

That fear reaction could leave you angry, bitter, depressed, and sick, as you saw from my earlier stories. That which you feared would happen in the first place can come upon you. Fear and faith work like self-fulfilling prophecies; you attract exactly by faith just what you hoped for, good or bad. Fear is not the way to deal with a life challenge. Fear is a limiting belief that works against us and gives us the very thing that we are not hoping for. So, what exactly is fear? Fear, like faith, is an emotional response to a futuristic state. Faith causes us to thoughtfully respond to a futuristic state. Unlike faith, fear causes us to react to the unknown, which is a futuristic state of being as well, without thinking. In the case of both fear and faith, we choose whether to react or respond; it is up to us. You have a choice to heed the admonition of Jesus, who tells us not to be afraid of tomorrow. Tomorrow, He says, will take care of itself. In other words, you cannot change tomorrow's outcome because you have no control over tomorrow's events. Here is what He encourages in John 16:33: "Do not be afraid, for I have overcome the world." And, Paul, following Jesus's advice in Philippians 4:6, warns us against anxiety. Instead, he encourages us to take every situation to God in prayer and do so with an attitude of thanksgiving, just as I did when I received the news of my husband's death. I took my fears to God in prayer and trusted in the power of the Divine Coach to help me live a life of faith instead of fear.

Jesus modeled for us the correct posture to respond to life-challenging situations and adversities. Jesus took authority over every challenging situation He confronted by faith. For example, when He met the blind, He spoke of healing simply by saying, "Be healed." When He encountered a great storm on the sea, He authoritatively spoke these words to the storm, "Peace be still." When he encountered death, He took authority over death and called forth the dead to life. Essentially, Jesus is asking us to follow His example. He asks us to respond in faith when faced with life challenges and not react in fear. In responding, we reflect on who we are, and we draw from the guidance and direction of the Divine Coach within. In other words, we go within to experience the unlimited potential we have been given to respond to life challenges. That's the essence of inside-out living.

Living life from the inside out is to experience the abundant, fulfilled, satisfied, and successful life of significance. That is the life Christ came to give us all. It is a life where we experience life in the Spirit. That life in the Spirit is evidenced by love, joy, peace, patience, gentleness, goodness, faithfulness, and self-control. It is the life that we experience when we live our lives from the inside out by the guidance of the Divine Coach within.

CHAPTER X

Intentional Living:
Taking Responsibility For Your Life

*Living a maximum potential life requires you to be intentional
about achieving your life dreams.*

Intentional living means taking responsibility for every area of your life. What do you believe about your potential? Do you believe you have unlimited potential, and if so, are you using that potential to the maximum? Each of us has been blessed with unlimited potential. The problem is that we are not aware of it, so it remains untapped. If our potential remains untapped, it will rob others of the value only you can add to them.

Intentional living requires you to take a deeper dive on the journey to discover the unlimited potential God has given you in order to live the abundant life that you desire. As you do so, let me ask you to consider three critical questions necessary for accessing your personal potential. These are the questions I had to ask myself as I faced the myriad of challenges I shared with you in the previous chapters.

1. How far are you willing to go to have that life of significance you
    are dreaming of living?

2. What sacrifices are you willing to make to access your unlimited potential so you have that life of fulfillment and significance that you desire?
3. What are the limiting beliefs standing in the way of expanding your personal potential to live a life of fulfillment and significance?

Responses to these questions will require you to reflect and take a journey within. And, if you are prepared to take the journey, to go all in, you will experience a life of serenity, fulfillment, and significance. So, let me ask you another question. How are you using the unlimited personal potential you have been given? You see, if that potential within you is left untapped, you will not only rob others of the value only you can add to them, but you will never realize what a great life you can have.

Living your life to its maximum potential will require you to live intentionally. It will require you to stretch yourself to grow beyond your current potential. To do so, you must put a personal growth plan in place. Do you have a personal growth plan? What are your personal, business, or professional growth plans for the next 3 – 6 months? What are the three biggest challenges standing in the way of achieving those plans? If you were speaking with me at the end of this year, what would have happened in your personal and professional life for you to say that this was an outstanding year, even a masterpiece year for you?

These three very important questions will require you to reflect, to go within, to search yourself to see whether you know who you are, whether you know where you are, whether you know what you want, whether you know what difference you want to make in this life, who will benefit and, finally, what sacrifices you are willing to make to have the abundant life you desire.

Living a maximum potential life requires you to be intentional about achieving your life dreams. In order to achieve my dreams, I had to be willing to go within and make personal sacrifices, and it wasn't easy. If you desire to live your life to its fullest, you must be willing to go within. You must be willing to reflect on who you are, where you are, where you want to go, and the sacrifices you must make to get there. To go within, you must first accept that you have unlimited potential within and must be willing to grow that potential.

Maximum potential (Intentional) living will require you to know and appreciate your unlimited potential and unique capability.It will require you to take the journey of reflection within. Let me now invite you to reflect for a moment on the next set of questions. It would be best if you find a quiet place to do so.

1. Are you willing to stretch yourself to grow beyond your comfort zone to experience maximum potential living?
2. Are you willing to stretch yourself and do something significant?
3. Are you willing to do something noble and purposeful with your life?

If the answer to the questions above is yes, you must go a little further in the journey within and shut out all voices in your external environment. Going within will allow you to hear the voice of the Holy Spirit, your Divine Coach. Now that you are totally focused within, you must be willing to trust that your Divine Coach knows what is best for you. The last step is to respond by applying the internal divine wisdom which comes from your Divine Coach. This is the essence of maximum potential (intentional) living and walking in the Spirit.

Choose to respond in the Spirit

Maximum potential (Intentional) living for the believer is seeking the guidance of the divine coach when faced with life's challenges and adversities and choosing to respond in obedience to His divine guidance. The Holy Spirit is the Spirit of Love and will always guide you to respond in love. 1 Corinthians 13:1-13 defines the way of love and provides us with a practical life application of walking in love. To walk in love doesn't mean that you have to act all super-spiritual, memorize a bunch of scriptures, show that you understand spiritual mysteries or that you have faith to move mountains. According to the Scriptures, walking in love is demonstrated practically, in essence, by treating others the way we want to be treated.

To walk in love is to show loving-kindness, patience, humility, and gentleness. When you walk in love, you do not rejoice when others are suffering or wish ill on others. Instead, it is to desire the best outcome for yourself and others. 1 Corinthians 13:4-13 states, *"Love is patient and kind; love does not envy or boast; it is not arrogant or rude. It does not insist on its own way; it is not irritable or resentful; 6 it does not rejoice at wrongdoing, but rejoices with the truth. Love bears all things, believes all things, hopes all things, endures all things. Love never ends."*

The Holy Spirit will manifest Himself within you with joy, peace, patience, gentleness, goodness, faithfulness, kindness, and self-control when you walk intentionally in love. He will always guide you to respond to whatever challenges you face with love. So, when responding in the spirit of obedience, He will empower you to let love, manifesting itself in all those character traits, guide your response in life's challenging situations. This love will empower you to be kind, patient, and gentle with yourself and others. Your response in the spirit will manifest itself at times with patience and understanding with self and others and also by being non-judgmental and forgiving. Love will mean practicing the golden rule: do unto others as you would have them do unto you. In short, walking in love means having the ability to be empathic. To be empathetic, you will need to step out of your comfort zone and challenge yourself to walk in someone else's shoes.

Walking in love is not easy; it is challenging. It will challenge your core life values and your personal integrity. Most of all, during life transitions, when changes, challenges, and adversities come your way, walking in love will challenge your commitment and dedication to doing the right thing just because it is the right thing to do. To do the right thing at the right time just because it is the right thing to do requires walking in the Spirit and partnering with the Divine Coach to access strategic divine wisdom. Strategic divine wisdom takes you from knowledge to understanding and from understanding to application. It is applied knowledge that will give you full access to the abundant life that Christ came to give you the life you so desire for yourself and your loved ones.

Practical Tips To Living Your Life from the Inside Out

Life doesn't give you what you want or what you desire. Life gives you who you are – you create your own life, and you do so by setting goals and taking intentional steps to live by your intentions. To be clear, you are the one who has to take those deliberate steps to have the life you want or to create the life you want. You do not leave it up to luck or chance or someone else to do it for you and make it happen. This is the essence of what I define as intentional living.

Intentional living requires that you take responsibility for your life outcomes. You are responsible for the life you have today and the life you will have in the future. If you want to experience maximum potential living, a life of abundance, success, prosperity, influence, and significance, you must take responsibility for your life outcomes. You can only do so by living your life from the inside out. Intentional living is taking action, that is, taking responsibility for your life outcomes. Taking action is the only way you and I will experience the abundant life that Christ came to give us.

You must take several intentional steps to live your life from the inside out. First, you have to take intentional steps to unlock the untapped potential that lies within your subconscious mind to create the life you want. Unlocking the power of your subconscious mind allows you to become that person who is capable of consciously creating the results you desire for yourself, rather than unconsciously recreating, time and time again, results you'd like to change. Next, you must identify your performance gap. Your performance gap is the gap between what you know and what you do on a day-to-day basis. Thirdly, it is critical that you take intentional steps to close your performance gap. Closing the performance gap will demand rigorous self-leadership and intentional self-discipline on your part. Your personal integrity, goals, and aspirations will be challenged. You will be challenged to change your thinking and your current narrative – that is how you label the life challenges and adversities that come your way. But, I promise you if you are willing to be intentional about all of the above, you will have the amazing life you desire. To have that life, here are some of the questions you must answer for yourself:

1. What kind of future do you want for you and your loved ones?
2. How is your current narrative restricting you from enjoying the life you want?
3. How willing are you to challenge your current narrative and personal integrity to put your self-leadership to the test to have the life you want?

Although Jesus assured us that He came to give us an abundant life, He also gave us values and guidelines, relational, physical, financial, personal, and spiritual laws that we must abide by to have that abundant life. So, what does that mean? It means that you and I have a part to play in accessing that abundant life. In other words, to have that abundant life, we must be intentional. Intentional living requires us to go within. On this journey, with the help of the Holy Spirit, our Divine Guide, we can reflect, plan and execute that plan.

The Holy Spirit won't do it alone. Despite the fact that Christ came to give us an abundant life, it is up to you and me to ensure that we intentionally cooperate with the person of the Holy Spirit by doing our part to have that life. We must practice intentional living to have that promised abundant, meaningful, fulfilled life. Here are four critical life principles for you to have that abundant life:

Principle #1: Intentional living requires that you go within to gain access to your God-given unlimited potential to be the best version of yourself. Every person has talents, skills, personality traits, and other characteristics that make up who they are. What are yours? Do you take them for granted, or do you value them? What can you draw upon to add value to others?

The answer to these questions requires you to know and appreciate your unique life experiences and capabilities. So, what's unique about you? How can you use your uniqueness and your unique life experiences to contribute to doing something noble and purposeful with your life?

There are people in your life who would greatly benefit from what you have to give. Are you aware of them? Are you being intentional about doing for them what you're suited to do? Can you think of someone you can add value to today based on your answer to these questions? What small but important shift can you make in your thinking and daily actions that will encourage you to prioritize helping others rather than promoting yourself? How do you think it will make you feel to place a greater emphasis on adding value to others using your best skills and talents? Think about your different relationships: at home, at work, and among friends – what person in your life right now would most benefit from you investing your talent with them? How can you make that happen? Specifically, identify your greatest skills and talents and who in your world would benefit most from investing those talents. Then review your ideas of how you can make that happen, and then take action.

Principle # 2: Intentional living requires developing a resilient mindset.

Intentional living requires willingness and commitment to developing a resilient mindset, which requires personal growth. And, how do you grow personally? You do so by leveraging all your life transition experiences to become the best version of yourself. One of the ways I leverage life transition experiences is by leaning on my faith and reflecting on the lessons I learn from all life experiences, whether they are good or bad. I am a firm believer in reflection. I have a very healthy prayer life, and most of my reflections occur when I am in meditation and prayer. I believe that before you plan the next twenty-four hours, you should reflect on the past twenty-four hours. So, I spend time on my knees every night before I go to bed, reflecting before the Lord on the day's performance. I repent where it is needed, give thanks where I need to, and praise and worship God as I reflect on the opportunities and blessings He provided for me to have such a great day. Most of my days are great; I've had very few difficult days. I have challenges just to stretch me enough to grow to the next level mentally and spiritually.

So, why would I reflect over the past day? I reflect over the past day to see what lessons I could learn. What did I do well? What could I have done better? Where did I miss it? I investigate and ask questions. In evaluating an experience, I am thinking about what I am thinking about. And, when I prod myself and ask myself questions like that, there comes a point where I receive divine illumination that helps me make good choices and informed life decisions. We receive valuable lessons and insights from the process of self-reflection. From that process of going within, you and I can develop a resilient mindset to live a maximum potential life.

Principle # 3: Intentional living requires developing a resilient mindset by going within.

If you fail to go within, you will go without maximum potential living. Developing resilience means that you must be willing and intentional to go within to listen to the Divine Coach for divine wisdom. You must have heard it said that experience is a great teacher. That statement is only partially correct – it is an evaluated experience of the past that is a great teacher. We learn from reflecting on our past experiences. As we ask our Divine Coach questions, He provides us with insights that the world cannot give us. The internal revelation that the Divine Coach provides strengthens our faith.

The Divine Coach reveals things to us in many different ways. We read many Biblical accounts of Him speaking to Prophets, the Apostles, and even to ordinary people in dreams and visions. He warned the Apostle Paul of impending danger to his life on many occasions. After the conflicts

Paul had in Philippi and Ephesus, he received threats of imprisonment and death. These threats were not idle, for indeed, two attempts were actually made on his life. He was taken into custody by the Roman government, and a case was brought against him, which, though false, ultimately led to his execution. Yet through it all, Paul maintained extraordinary courage.

Despite the threats, he continued preaching the gospel and even dared to preach to the Jewish and Roman captors. In the end, his courage proves decisive, not only for his work of preaching the gospel but for saving the lives of hundreds of people in the midst of a shipwreck. His own words sum up his attitude of courage as those around him shrink back in fear: "What are you doing, weeping and breaking my heart? For I am ready not only to be bound but even to die in Jerusalem for the name of the Lord Jesus" (Acts 21:13 ESV).

The point, however, is not that Paul was a man of extraordinary courage but that the Holy Spirit gives each of us the inner resilience we need to do our work. Paul credits the Holy Spirit for keeping him going in the face of such adversity.

"When they arrived, he said to them: You know how I lived the whole time I was with you, from the first day I came into the province of Asia. I served the Lord with great humility and with tears and in the midst of severe testing by the plots of my Jewish opponents. You know that I have not hesitated to preach anything that would be helpful to you but have taught you publicly and from house to house. I have declared to both Jews and Greeks that they must turn to God in repentance and have faith in our Lord Jesus. "And now, compelled by the Spirit, I am going to Jerusalem, not knowing what will happen to me there. I only know that in every city the Holy Spirit warns me that prison and hardships are facing me. However, I consider my life worth nothing to me; my only aim is to finish the race and complete the task the Lord Jesus has given me—the task of testifying to the good news of God's grace.

The next morning some Jews formed a conspiracy and bound themselves with an oath not to eat or drink until they had killed Paul. More than forty men were involved in this plot. They went to the chief priests and the elders and said, "We have taken a solemn oath not to eat anything until we have killed Paul. Now then, you and the Sanhedrin petition the commander to bring him before you on the pretext of wanting more accurate information about his case. We are ready to kill him before he gets here"

(Acts 20:22;21:4; 23:L1 NIV).

These are only some of the life-challenging experiences Paul faced in carrying out the call of God in his life. Yet, his internal response to those experiences was always to seek the Holy Spirit's guidance, not to fear what was happening in the external environment. Paul's experiences encourage believers today that we can also depend on the Holy Spirit to give us the inner resilience and courage we may lack to respond to impending danger.

Today, the Divine Coach continues to reveal impending danger to believers. However, He only does that to those who are intentional about developing an intimate relationship with Him. We must be intentional about tuning out the external environment, the voice of the world, and go within to listen to His voice. We must also be intentional about seeking the Divine Coach for courage, guidance, and deliverance from within. Remember, if we fail to go within, we will go without.

It is quite tempting for believers to listen to the voices of the external environment when life challenges come our way, but we do not take our directions from the outside world. The answer and solutions to life's challenges are found within you and me. The scriptures confirm that greater is He (the Divine Coach) that is within us than He (the devil) that is operating in this dark and evil world. Although we are in the world, we are not of this world. We are the light of the world and the salt of the earth. We bring light to the current spiritual darkness in the world. The world is supposed to take directions from us.

When the world is confused and afraid, we bring clarity and provide direction to events that baffle the world like what took place on September 9th, 2001. I remember telling my friends and family about a dream I had on August 28th, 2001. In that dream there were two large buildings of similar heights. I was in one of them. The other was directly across from me. As I looked, the one that was directly across from the one in which I was standing imploded. Then, the one in which I was standing started to shake vehemently from the foundation. I knew that I was in great danger and would even die if I did not get out immediately. Fortunately, a divine hand as it were lifted the entire floor I was in and placed it safely onto the ground and I stepped out of a broken window. At the time, I did not know that I was receiving divine revelation about the events of 911 from the Holy Spirit. From these and many other dreams, I have learned that when life's challenges and adversities shore up, even life devastating events such as 911, instead of reacting to the outside environment the world did, I must go within and consult with the Holy Spirit, my Divine Coach to provide me with divine guidance.

Principle #4: Intentional Living results in maximum potential living.

It is my experience that intentional living results in maximum potential living. Living intentionally will help you develop the resilient mindset you need to be all that God has called you to be and do. To illustrate, I will share a personal experience of how intentional living has resulted in maximum potential living for me.

As I write this chapter, sitting in my home office in Mount Vernon, Alexandria, I've been reminiscing a little bit today. I've been thinking back over the years and just observing my own journey, now in retrospect. I'm definitely still on this journey and will be until the day I die. Yet, I think it's always good to take some time to reflect on how far I've come and to take a moment to celebrate.

I am so grateful for the many mentors and coaches who have poured into me, who have added value to me, thereby evoking the unlimited potential God has blessed me with. I remember when I first came to the USA, I was leaving a broken marriage and about to start life all over again at age 37. Looking back, all I could depend on was my resilient faith in God. Although I had a four-year degree from a Bible College, a Bachelors in Linguistics, and a visitor's visa status in the USA, there was not much I could do with these without a work permit or a permanent resident status. Since I had no intention of returning to the Caribbean, an environment where I was not thriving, I needed to find a job so that I could continue to live in the USA and support myself. At that stage of my life, I was stepping into new territory in my dream building, and to be honest, although I was a woman of faith and trusted God to take care of me, there was a big part of me that was afraid. I didn't know the first thing of how to get US permanent resident visa status, let alone how I would find a job. I wanted to go back to school, own a home, and most importantly, I wanted to have my only son move here to be with me. I had big dreams that felt impossible, but I was convinced that with the resilient faith I inherited from my grandmother, I could overcome my fears and I would make it.

I remembered following my Divine Coach's voice and calling a friend I had met in Latin America. I shared with her what I was experiencing and the big dreams I had. She invited me to come to Washington, DC, to spend the weekend with her. She encouraged me to bring all my personal and academic documents with me. I remembered her saying to me, "You will be surprised by the response you will get here in DC," and I was surprised.

Going to DC was the best move I had made since coming to the US. I submitted job applications to three organizations, and all three of them offered me a job. With much prayer, consultation, intentionality, and much focus on my dreams, I accepted the job that I felt would help me accomplish those dreams. I was right. I had made the right decision. With the help of that organization, I received my US residency status with permission to live and work in the USA. One year later, I met my late husband and enrolled in a Graduate Program at Johns Hopkins University.

Two years later, I bought my first home, five years later, I remarried, and six years later, I had finished two Master's Degrees and a Ph.D. Looking back, I am amazed at how fast it all happened.

I don't want you to think that there were no challenges along the way because there were many. There was a divorce, and there were deaths. Remember I said I had left an abusive marriage, and during those transition years, I also lost my grandmother, who raised me, and my first grandchild got ill and died. So, there was pain, disappointment, sacrifices, and financial challenges.

Getting a divorce and starting over again was not easy. I was working full-time and going to school at night part-time. At times, I didn't think I would make it. I had to respond to the many voices in my external environment, like well-meaning family members and friends who didn't believe I was doing the right thing and the voices of fear, doubt, and insecurity in my internal environment. There was also the voice of self-judgment; it creeps up on us so quickly and so easily, doesn't it?

Though I am a woman of faith, another part of me didn't believe in my unlimited potential. At times, I didn't have enough faith to keep going and pursue my dreams. It is amazing how limiting beliefs could stand in the way of attaining the abundant life we so desire. Fortunately, I had spiritual mentors and coaches who helped me cast my vision of what I wanted my future to look like. You see, although you are graced with unlimited potential, you have within you both the voice of fear and the voice of belief, the voice of doubt and the voice of faith. Unless you have a personal, intimate relationship with the Divine Coach, it is very easy to go in the wrong direction. Fortunately, I learned to trust His guidance over the years and not let doubt and limiting beliefs prevent me from accomplishing my goals and fulfilling my life calling. You too must endeavor to establish a partnership with the Divine Coach and trust Him. Trust Him to help you step fully into your divine calling so that you can live a maximum potential life. That is my prayer for each one of you, my readers.

CHAPTER XI

Unlocking Your Inner Power

There's a process and a system for you to follow to get from where you are right now to where you want to be.

As we close out our time together, I want to leave you with some last thoughts and reflections. If I were to ask you when you hear the word 'dream,' what is the first thing that comes to mind? Most of you would reference Dr. Martin Luther King's famous speech, *I have a dream.* Having a dream and believing in it is perhaps one of the most powerful responses to life challenges and adversities. Dr. King's response to the life challenge of racism in this country was definitely an example of an appropriate response to one of life's challenges. Even though he didn't live to see his dream fulfilled, his response to that challenge of racial discrimination continues to positively impact our lives even today.

There is another person that impacted my life so positively that it led me to write this book. Viktor Frankl had what I call an impossible dream; he was a professor when he was imprisoned. He dreamed of being released from prison and returning to his classroom, and he was able to do so based on his mindset about his response to life challenges and adversities. Unlike Dr. King, Victor Frankl lived to see his dream fulfilled.

Frankl believed that when life challenges show up, every person has a response ability. He believed that it is in the power of every human being to either respond or react to life challenges and that no one can take away from us the personal power or ability which resides inside each of us. Frankl documented his response to the challenges and adversities he suffered while imprisoned in a German concentration camp at the hands of the German Nazis in his classic book: *Man's Search for Meaning: An Introduction to Logotherapy.*[10]

Frankl tells how he was able to use his "response-ability" while he was in captivity, being persecuted day and night by his captors. Every day they tortured him, and he forgave them each time. He related that the only thing they could not take away from him was his ability to respond versus reacting to their abuse. So day and night, no matter how often they tortured him, he maintained his "response-ability." They could not force him to respond the way they wanted. Instead, it was within his power to determine how he would respond. He chose instead to forgive them when they were torturing him.

Another powerful thing he did while he was tortured and throughout his stay in the camp was to believe that he would get out of there one day. So daily, he pictured himself standing in the classroom in front of his students. He went so far as to write what he was going to say to them when he got out.He was going to share with them how he withstood the pain and the torture of imprisonment. He would share with them how his resilient mindset contributed to him getting out of prison. He fixed his mind on what he wanted to accomplish, and he removed all traces of unforgiveness from his mind to the extent that he learned to love those who were abusing him.

Frankl found the answer to living an abundant life by living his life from the inside out. He chose to go inside to access the resilience with which he was empowered to respond to life challenges and adversities. He found the power of the Holy Spirit, the Divine Coach, who empowered

---

[10] Viktor E. Frankl, *Man's Search for Meaning,* (Boston, Beacon Press, 2006)

him to respond to his torturers with love and helped him to maintain hope in a difficult situation.

No matter how difficult the challenge you are facing, through the power of the Holy Spirit, you are able to respond appropriately, like Viktor Frankl, Dr. Martin Luther King, Joseph in the Bible, and my friend Mary. That is the power of your "response-ability," which lies deep within you. You can choose to respond to life challenges rather than react. With the power of the Holy Spirit, your Divine Coach, you can choose to live your life from the inside out.

By now, you must realize that creating the life you want is no easy feat. It depends on how you use your thoughts, imagination, and faith in combination. Sadly, many people are compounding their own misery, be it the constant struggle, the "stuckness" of stagnation and the frustration coming from it, or the trappings of a successful business, increasingly consuming almost every hour of their life.

As much as they desperately want better outcomes: more money, better health, more time and richer relationships with significant others, a better environment in which to live or work, more time to engage in the passions that make life so rewarding, it is fleeting, if it ever transpires. Not because they're incapable of making it happen, but because they never deal with what's causing it all. Understandably so, because no one's educated in how to do it. So, for the relatively small percentage, aware enough to seek growth, and fuller expression, through the only way possible, self-improvement. Instead, they routinely do what they've been programmed to do by the environment of their upbringing and a so-called "education" system that's based on an entirely flawed understanding of the human psyche and potential. So, they bombard their intellect with data and information: they read and consume a plethora of books, they attend motivation seminars, and "skill up" on training courses, all of which, regardless of the quality of content, do next to nothing, in terms of making tangible and substantial improvements a reality in their lives.

Understand this, the potential you're not currently expressing in your life, often referred to as your "untapped potential" will NEVER be found in your intellect. Nothing much will improve in your life because what you know and what you do are poles apart. So, you can continue to exercise your intellect by absorbing all the data and information you like, and you'll ONLY be a "paragon of knowledge."

I don't think I need to explain that if what you do doesn't change, neither will the results you're creating in your life. Do you realize that it is quite possible for you to store up in your mind a million facts and be entirely uneducated? Unless you change your behavior and put into practice what you learned, the information and the facts will remain dormant. Unless you use it, you will lose it. So, in fact, to be educated doesn't mean teaching people what they do not know; it means teaching them to change their behavior, that is, to behave differently.

So what does all this mean for you? You will agree with me that I am just skimming the surface of inside out living here in this book. I believe that some of you will want to continue to go deeper into unlocking your untapped unlimited potential after reading this book. So, I invite you to a new understanding of the word "education" , the one true to the meaning associated with the Latin root of the word "educo" meaning "to draw out."[11] I invite you to the education that perhaps you never received - the one that will help you to unlock the untapped potential you must unlock if you're to become the person capable of making your future goals, aspirations, and dreams a reality, should you desire to embrace it.

You are, of course, free to ignore the great truths shared with you in this book. You always have a choice, whether you're aware of it or not, and you're free to make any choice you wish, however, by the unwavering assertion of another natural law, cause and effect. You cannot escape the consequences of your choices. So, the question you have to ask yourself is, what part of you are you going to feed? What part of you are you going to nurture and cultivate? For most of us, our programmed default is to err on the side of doubt and fear, but the beautiful thing about humankind is that we've each been given the ability to choose.

---

[11] "Educo Definition & Meaning,"World of Dictionary
https://worldofdictionary.com/dict/latin-english/meaning/educo, (accessed 11/30/21)

You don't have to live the way you were originally programmed as a young child and up to the point where you are now in your life. At any given point, you can choose to turn the switch on the radio and tune into a different station. So, which voice are you going to listen to? Are you going to hold onto the belief within you and keep watering it, providing it with the nutrients it needs to grow? Or will you allow the voices of fear and doubt to squelch it and grow over it like weeds in a garden?

Today, I can say that I have the life I want; I am living my best life now! Life's opportunities have come in the form of challenges and adversities, and I didn't get here by accident. It wasn't by luck that I was able to create what I have in my life. And I don't say that to boast, but to share with you this fact, the process I followed was a lawful process that works for anyone who will follow it. I live by the causality principle: you reap what you sow. That simply means that I am the co-creator of my life outcomes. To have the outcome I want, I have to invest in my personal growth and partner with the Holy Spirit. My ultimate goal is to expand the Kingdom of God and bring glory to God.

Since I began my personal growth journey, I haven't stopped growing. I have been and continue to intentionally invest in my personal growth and in the lives of others. Adding value to people's lives, particularly Kingdom leaders, has been my lifelong passion. I love to see God's people moving from one level of growth and from one level of greatness to another. Today, I am still as excited as I was in my early developmental years about my personal growth for the purpose of expanding the Kingdom of God. I do so by coaching Kingdom leaders, supporting them to maximize their leadership potential, and partnering with other Kingdom thought leaders to leave a legacy behind by training the next generation of Kingdom leaders. Now, I coach, mentor, speak and teach all about this in the various studies, books, courses, and programs that I provide.

There's a process and a system for you to follow to get from where you are right now to where you want to be. It will enable you to close the performance gap discussed earlier in the book, allowing you to move from what you know to what you do on a day-to-day basis. That process and system will require a specific mindset, one that is dedicated to self-discipline or self-control, commitment, consistency, accountability, coachability, lifelong learning, and gratitude. Below is a discussion on each one of these.

Self-Discipline or Self Control

The idea of self-discipline may be foreign to many, though the idea of self-control is not. The two are essentially the same. God highly esteems self-control as it is part of the fruit of the Spirit along with love, joy, peace, patience, kindness, goodness, faithfulness, and gentleness (Galatians 5:22-23). It is this fruit that God is producing in His children.

Self-control as a Fruit of the Spirit is a bit of a paradox. How can the ability to control oneself result from being controlled by someone else? Two things are worth mentioning here. First, "fruit" here does not refer to individual items. It refers to a general outcome or result. The result of the Holy Spirit working in a person's life is love, joy, and all the rest. The second thing to note is that these are the results of the Holy Spirit. They are not the product of hard work or self-improvement. The believer must cooperate with the Holy Spirit, but it is still the Holy Spirit doing the work in us and through us.

It is helpful that in Galatians 5:19–21, Paul lists the Fruit of the Spirit. He also provides a differing list that describes the behavior of the one who is not living by the Holy Spirit, which he calls the actions of the flesh. Paul writes, "Now the works of the flesh are evident: sexual immorality, impurity, sensuality, idolatry, sorcery, enmity [hatred], strife [conflict], jealousy, fits of anger, rivalries, dissensions, divisions, envy, drunkenness, orgies, and things like these. As I warned you before, I warn you that those who do such things will not inherit the Kingdom of God."

In other words, those who allow these desires to control their behaviors will not experience the benefits of a spirit-filled life, one guided by the Divine Coach. That believer lacks self-control, which is the one fruit of the Spirit that undergirds the other eight: love, peace, patience, faithfulness, kindness, gentleness, goodness, and forbearance. Self-control is required to obey the dictates of the Divine Coach.

Do we like self-control? Generally, no. Humans don't like any control placed on us, whether by ourselves, others, or God. God knows this, and we learn in Hebrews 12:11 that, "For the moment all discipline seems painful rather than pleasant, but later it yields the peaceful fruit of righteousness to those who have been trained by it." All discipline seems painful, whether it is a correction from a loving dad or when your boss points out your mistake, a conviction from the Holy Spirit when we sin, when we choose to restrain our desires for the wellbeing of others, or when we delay gratification for a better outcome later. We tend to hate self-discipline because we choose not to do what we want to do, or just the opposite, choosing to do what we do not want to do. The believer who desires to overcome life's challenges and adversities must submit to the disciplines of the Holy Spirit, our Divine Coach. In fact, the only way a believer is identified as a child of God is by living a disciplined life evidenced by the outward manifestation of the Fruit of the Spirit.

We are thus encouraged in Hebrews 12: 5-9 about the virtue of discipline: "My son, do not make light of the Lord's discipline, and do not lose heart when he rebukes you, because the Lord disciplines the one he loves, and he chastens everyone he accepts as his son. Endure hardship as discipline; God is treating you as his children. For what children are not disciplined by their father? If you are not disciplined—and everyone undergoes discipline—then you are not legitimate, not true sons and daughters at all. Moreover, we have all had human fathers who disciplined us and we respected them for it. How much more should we submit to the Father of spirits and live!"

These days, it may be hard to know what self-discipline looks like in a practical sense, but it is easy to know what the lack of self-discipline looks like. All we need to do is read the newspaper, watch the evening news on most television stations, and read and see stories of people living with no self-discipline whatsoever. We read reports and watch stories of violence, satanic rituals, drunk driving, theft, and drug abuse, and the list goes on.

Paul tells us that we should walk by the dictates of the Holy Spirit, and in that way, we will not gratify the desires of the flesh (Galatians 5:16). The world does not walk by the Spirit or is expected to do so because it does not know the Spirit of God nor cannot receive Him, but believers know Him and must commit themselves to walk in obedience to Him.

Consistency

Being consistent means fully dedicating yourself completely to a task, activity, or goal. It means to fully stay engaged without distraction and be faithful to what is important. One of the characteristics of God is that He is faithful. Our goal as believers is to stay engaged without distraction as we build an intimate relationship with God. It means that we ought to be faithful to God as He is faithful to us. That is why we need to develop the fruit of faithfulness in our walk with God. The Apostle Paul reminds us that even if we are faithless, He remains faithful, for He cannot disown Himself (2 Timothy 2:13).

Consistency is the key to close relationships in our everyday lives and our spiritual lives. Consistency in our time with God starts with simple changes, but those simple changes can make a big impact. First, you must find time to be alone. Set aside time in your busy schedules to spend time with God every day without distractions. Consistency is equivalent to being faithful and committed to the call of God in your life. God is always working in our lives, but if we don't spend time tuning our hearts to the voice of our Divine Coach within, we will miss when He speaks. Do you want to grow closer to God? Be consistent in seeking Him daily.

Commitment

Commitment speaks of a lifestyle of self-control. It means that you have discovered something that you believe in, you want it badly enough, and so you have determined in your mind that no matter what, you will dedicate your life to being successful at whatever that thing or goal is.

A life lived in the spirit is radically different from a life lived under the dictates of the desires of the flesh. It is a life imbued with wisdom, grace, and virtue. Living this life calls for commitment to walking in obedience. With that committed mindset, the believer longs to do God's will and live according to His edicts and can do so because he/she is consistently under control of the Holy Spirit and does not follow selfish desires.

It is a radical lifestyle that only a few people are willing to make the sacrifice and develop the discipline to lean into. It is a life that can only be successfully lived with a coach, mentor, or accountability partner. It is a life that the Holy Spirit must guide, and most believers find it only by walking in close collaboration with the Holy Spirit.

Accountability

Being accountable to another person requires trust, humility, and submission. Only the Divine Coach can empower the believer to develop these character traits. Therefore, your life in the spirit requires walking closely with the Divine Coach, who is your divine accountability partner. He guides you into developing that relationship of trust and submission with another believer.

Having another believer as an accountability partner is critical to you both living a spirit-filled life. You both establish the relationship for the sake of mutual edification and exhortation to avoid sinful behaviors. You hold each other "accountable" – that is, you honestly report to each other for the goals you set for yourself, and each of you considers yourself answerable to the other.

Too many believers try to do life alone, but you don't have to, for we are relational beings. The scripture says in Genesis 2:18, "It is not good that man should be alone; I will make him a helper comparable to him." You need a helper, an accountability partner to help you in the areas of life or your business that you find most challenging. Two believers can accomplish more than one. You will discover that an accountability partner is just what you need to help you break habits that you have struggled to break for many years. Many alcoholics and food addicts seek out support groups where accountability partners are assigned as mentors to aid the addict in overcoming addiction. This requires a willingness on the part of the sufferer to submit to that assigned accountability partner or mentor.

Believers who are filled with the Holy Spirit find themselves struggling with addictive behaviors also. Once identified, that believer must admit to the addiction and be willing to seek out an accountability partner for support. The believer who is willing to seek out and submit to another believer as an accountability partner for help with hard to break habits or to receive mentoring support in any challenging area of life must first be willing to submit to and receive guidance from the Holy Spirit before entering into that accountability partnering relationship.

Coachability

Coaching is one of the most transformational relationships that anyone could ever experience. Coaching is designed to help the person entering into that relationship grow, change, transform, and improve or excel in specifically identified areas of life. Being coachable means that you are ready to do what it takes to experience that transformation and change. Ideally, entering into a coaching relationship with a qualified professional coach will help you unlock your hidden and untapped potential allowing you to become the best version of yourself you were created to be.

I have always had a coach; coaching has helped me to grow. It has helped me identify the belief systems that undermine my attaining success in life. I have been able to identify limiting beliefs, thoughts, behaviors, and character traits, including the familial cultures and customs that were impeding my continuous growth and standing in the way of me developing into the best version of myself. These are some of the major benefits of coaching.

Coaching is not mentoring, therapy, or counseling. It may include some of these aspects, but coaching in its purest form empowers and transforms. In fact, having an academic, leadership, and business coach have transformed my life. In addition to a Ph.D. dissertation committee which is generally assigned by the university, I needed a coach to take me through the daunting dissertation process. I also engaged a financial coach to support me with investing in the stock market. A coach supported me in setting up the Zorbas Orphans Fund, the nonprofit organization I founded twelve years ago to provide higher education to orphans and vulnerable youths between the ages of fourteen and twenty-five. I wanted to help them take care of themselves during their adult years, contribute to their nations' socio-economic development, and negotiate at a higher level in society. I would not have been able to write and complete this book had it not been for the help of my book writing coach.

Do you desire to unlock your full potential? Begin your journey to a better you with coaching that's fundamentally human, tailored to you. Start your free coaching trial now! I will provide more information on how you can enter into that transformational relationship with me in the conclusion section of the book.

Lifelong Learning

Lifelong learning is the ongoing, voluntary, and self-motivated pursuit of knowledge for personal or professional reasons. Therefore, it enhances social inclusion, active citizenship, personal development, self-sustainability, competitiveness, and employability.

I consider myself a lifelong learner because of my curious nature. Although I started working at age fifteen, I continued to engage in adult education for self-sustainability and relevancy as well as competitiveness and employability. I completed my Doctoral degree at age 48 and became a Certified IFC Coach through the Georgetown University Leadership Coaching Certification Program. It was one of the many transformational learning experiences I have had.

I also wanted to learn how to manage my own investment portfolio to grow my money, so I took classes in real estate investing, stocks, and trading in stock options. I even studied for the Series Six exam, which is the exam investment brokers and financial advisors have to pass in order to manage an investment portfolio. I did that because I wanted to increase my knowledge of how money works in a capitalist society and, at the same time, explore other areas where I could invest my money.

One of the unique advantages of continuous learning through the many adult education programs I immersed myself in is sharing the journey with people of all backgrounds. Not only do I have my own personal and professional experiences to bring to the table, but I can also learn from the experiences of classmates and professors from around the country and world.

Continuous learning for the adult learner brings a well-rounded perspective that can be valuable in your business and personal life. You'll typically collaborate with peers on team projects, assignments, or discussion threads in many learning environments. By sharing your ideas and receiving feedback from classmates and faculty, you have the opportunity to gain a global perspective on complex issues.

I continue to expand my mental capacity because of my curious nature and thirst for knowledge, which I believe can only be satisfied through continuous learning. This continuous learning mindset has helped me be a very resourceful coach and mentor to my clients as I can add value to them in multiple dimensions of their lives through the divine guidance of the Holy Spirit, my Divine Coach.

Gratitude

I started off this book by asking you how you perceived life challenges and adversities. I suggested that your perception of life challenges and adversities will determine whether you respond or react to them. So, I asked you to examine whether you respond or react to them because your response or your reaction will then determine the outcome you derive. I now encourage you to take a deeper dive inside and consider a very important principle that will change your life as we come to the end of this book, the principle of gratitude.

Gandhi has always said, "Be the change you want to see in this world." But few people really know the meaning of that. He was referring to the power of changing your perception, and the key to changing your perception and living a more fulfilling life is to practice gratitude. Unfortunately, this word has been thrown around so much that it has lost its meaning. So what is gratitude?

As children, the first thing our elders teach us is to say "thank you." Most times, children would just blurt out "thank you" for fear of punishment without knowing its meaning and power. As young as I could remember, I had to say "thank you" when I was given anything, or else, it would be held back until I said the magic phrase. I was taught at an early age to say grace before meals. Grace before meals meant that we had to thank God, who provided the meals to us before we could eat. No matter how hungry I was, I could not touch that food until I said grace; I continue that practice today. I don't only thank God for my meals, I thank God for everything He has blessed me with. As believers, we give thanks to God for everything He has blessed us with, materially, relationally, financially, personally, physically, and spiritually. So, the mindset of gratitude was drilled into me at a very early age. As a result, as a young mother, the first thing I taught my son was the principle of gratitude because I wanted to pass it on to my children.

So, let me ask you this. What comes to mind when you hear the word gratitude? What do you think about gratitude? Do you say "thank you" when someone does an act of kindness for you? Do you say "thank you" when you get a salary increase? While these can be counted as gratitude, it barely scratches the surface when it comes to transforming your life; they are only short-lived.

Gratitude is an attitude of the heart or the spirit. It is an attitude that is developed only from walking in partnership with the Holy Spirit. Living a life of gratitude is the will of God for every believer. We are encouraged to give thanks from a grateful heart, not for fear that we will be punished or not blessed if we don't. Gratitude has the power to transform your life.

Many people live a miserable life because they are not content. They are not grateful for what they have already been blessed with. They complain because they compare themselves with others, and they get jealous because they are not doing as well. Some people are easily disturbed by small, petty things, and challenges and adversities would paralyze them. Sure, many of them will be able to go through the motions and smile when they are supposed to or say thank you at the right time, but there is no meaning or truth behind it. Many believers are unhappy on the inside; they are broken, hollow, and hopeless, and that is because they have not been able to develop a relationship with the Greater One who lives inside of them, the Holy Spirit.

The gift of gratitude is one of the benefits of developing a relationship with the Holy Spirit to unlock all the hidden potential in your life. That relationship with the Holy Spirit will transform your heart into a heart of gratitude. That heart of gratitude will bring back all the energy and spark that has been missing in your life for so long. A heart of gratitude will cause you to be more productive and cause you to achieve the success in life you always wanted. An attitude of gratitude will allow you to see things in a new light. You will be able to see opportunities in every challenge and adversity and the beauty in every situation. A heart of gratitude will remove that feeling of doom and gloom. It removes fear, doubt, insecurity, anxiety, tension, and depression. In short, with an attitude of gratitude, you will experience a life of wholeness, peace, and joy in the Holy Spirit. You will be living your life from the inside out.

We have been experiencing an escalation of perilous times on the earth, and believers are not exempt from these adversities and challenges. There will be challenges from without, and still more, on account of corruption from within. The good news for every believer is that we can overcome these challenges and adversities if we respond to them rather than react. We do so through the strengthening process which the Holy Spirit of Christ takes us through. It is His promise to pour His Spirit on all flesh, especially in these last days where life's challenges and adversities can be overwhelming. Here is what the Prophet Joel says about this promise in Joel 2:28-29, "And it shall come to pass afterward, that I will pour out my spirit upon all flesh; and your sons and your daughters shall prophesy, your old men shall dream dreams, your young men shall see visions: And also upon the servants and upon the handmaids in those days will I pour out my spirit."

The passages in Joel 2:22-27, which precede this promise of the outpouring of the Holy Spirit, also hold some amazing benefits for the believer who demonstrates the courage to trust in the amazing power of God through the Holy Spirit. We must demonstrate our faith in His promise to take care of us no matter the challenges and adversities we may be experiencing. They include blessing on land, animals, and all that we possess.

Despite these amazing promises, we are not to be ignorant of the perilous times that the Apostle Paul warned us about and which evidently are already here on the earth. In 2 Timothy 3:1-5, Paul writes, "But mark this: There will be terrible times in the last days. People will be lovers of themselves, lovers of money, boastful, proud, abusive, disobedient to their parents, ungrateful, unholy, without love, unforgiving, slanderous, without self-control, brutal, not lovers of the good, treacherous, rash, conceited, lovers of pleasure rather than lovers of God having a form of godliness but denying its power."

And, we do need to have an intimate experience with the Holy Spirit in these last days to be able to respond to the perilous times Paul describes in the aforementioned scripture. Indeed, in these last days, we see humans who are not led by the Spirit who love to gratify their lusts more than pleasing God and walking in their calling and purpose. However, as a believer, you were created for a life of significance and greatness that is aligned to your calling so that you can make an impact in this world. The only way to accomplish that, especially in these perilous times, is with the help of your Divine Coach within, the Holy Spirit.

Let me take you back to the questions I asked you at the beginning of the book. What is your perspective on the life challenges and adversities you face in this life? Do you view life as presenting opportunities and options and that it is up to you to choose the outcome you want? Do you respond in faith, like my friend Mary did, who leveraged her son's death to transform her life into the best version of herself? Or, do you respond in fear, like my Aunt Leanna? If you recall, unlike my friend Mary, Auntie Leanna allowed the death of her husband to paralyze her with fear. She could never see the opportunity life was presenting her through this adversity to receive love from others, and, as far as I know, she never forgave God for taking her husband from her. Instead she lived the rest of her life complaining about how cruel God was to take her husband away from her, leaving her loveless and childless. As a result, she could not accept our help or our love; she complained to the bitter end. She reacted to life and allowed the life challenge to leave her bitter instead of responding in faith and being transformed into a better person.

How often are we faced with life's challenges and adversities, and our default reaction is to see the challenge and the adversity as the worst thing that could happen to us. In some cases, we look for someone to blame, and if there is no one to blame, we blame God. We question His motives, and we reason that if God allowed that to happen, He obviously doesn't love us. Why did that happen to me? Perhaps God is punishing me. We have become so used to a punitive society that as soon as a life challenge or adversity occurs, we attribute the challenge to God punishing us for something bad we did. We judge God by the way man treats us.

At the beginning of the book, the old man in our story was careful not to lean on his own understanding. Could it be that he was aware that his life had a purpose such that nothing in his life was a coincidence, that there was a purpose to everything that happened? That every incident in his life and the life of his son was meant to take him to his divine destiny. While the villagers saw challenges and adversities, he saw opportunities presented to make him into the best version of himself.

What about you? When you are faced with life's challenges, do you lean on your understanding? What is your perspective on what is going on in your life right now? Do you attribute it to bad luck? Or do you go within to seek the perspective of your Divine Coach, the Holy Spirit, so that He will give you a spiritual perspective, thereby allowing you to respond instead of react?

You can have the fulfilled, meaningful abundant life Christ came to guarantee you, but you must access it on the inside. Remember, life doesn't give you what you want; life gives you who you are. And, if you fail to go within, you will go without. So, go ahead, give yourself permission to live your life from the inside out by accessing the power of the Divine Coach within.

CONCLUSION

As I come to the end of this book, let me challenge you to be intentional about your personal growth so that you can maximize your potential, become the best version of yourself and live a life of significance for the glory of God. Will you trust yourself enough to step out, to take action, even in the face of fear? Will you hold firm to the belief and faith that you deserve all that you desire in your life, that you're worthy of it, and that you were created to enjoy the abundance and prosperity of this world? You have unlimited potential. Tap into it and experience the abundance your unlimited potential is waiting to express to the world through you, but you must be intentional.

If the answer to the questions above is yes, I invite you to join me in my online webinars or in my live coaching and mentoring sessions to learn to live your life from the inside out. As your Transformational Mindset and Life Transition Coach, I will come alongside you and guide you into accessing the power of the Divine Coach within you, thereby allowing you to unlock your untapped potential. If you are to become the person capable of making your goals, aspirations, and dreams for your life a reality, then your potential must be unlocked.

If that is your desire, simply indicate that to me by sending an email to: m.mcintoshalberts@gmail.com

Or, access the link below from your internet browser, leave your information and I will take care of the rest: www.calendly.com/m-mcintoshalberts.

Throughout this book, my desire was to encourage you to obtain that life of greatness in the Spirit by believing in yourself, in your divine calling, and your life purpose. I want to thank you for purchasing a copy of this book and for haven gotten this far into reading it. I hope you have gotten a clearer understanding of who the Divine Coach is and that you would get to know Him better. I believe in you, and I believe in your dream! Step confidently into your divine calling and maximize your life potential by living your life from the inside out!

ACKNOWLEDGEMENTS

First and foremost, I must give honor and glory to God for giving me the courage to complete this book.

Since this book is about the Holy Spirit, my Divine Coach, I must acknowledge and give thanks to Him because it is He who inspired and empowered me to contribute to extending the body of Biblical research on who He is, what His role is in the lives of Believers and how we can partner with Him to live the abundant life Christ came to ensure that we have.

Next, in order of importance, I want to give thanks to and honor my late grandmother, Jane McIntosh, for raising me to become the resilient woman of faith I have become. Her mentoring and coaching taught me that we are gifted with amazing unlimited power to live the life of our dreams. She instilled in me that whatever we sow in this life, we will reap an abundant harvest right here. It was from her I learned the principle that life doesn't give us what we want, it gives us who we are. She taught me to tap into my inner divine potential and live my life from the inside out, not from the outside in.

With this work, I also want to honor my late husband, Wim Alberts, who believed in me, and added tremendous value to me by supporting me in fulfilling my life dreams while he was still here with me physically. Before he died, he exacted a commitment from me to return to my divine calling, one of which is to share with the world the impact of my faith on my lived experiences. It is that faith in God that has empowered me to respond to life's challenges and adversities instead of reacting to them.

My special thanks to my son, Paul Buckmire, who is my greatest cheerleader, emotional, spiritual support, and prayer partner in this world. Paul, I love you so much. You may not know this, but you helped me to complete this book just by loving me through all of life's challenges, adversities and changes. This Book is dedicated to you. This book is also dedicated to the love of your life and my dear daughter-in-law Micelle, and my grandson, Aidan. You all mean the world to me. Thanks for your love and all your support, especially during these 13 years of widowhood. God bless you for all you do for me.

Words cannot express how grateful I am to my dear spiritual mentor and friend, Reverend Niyi Adams, for the integral role he has played in my life, not only in encouraging me and praying for me as I wrote this book but for mentoring and counseling me as I faced and responded to the many challenges life presents. His spiritual mentoring, Biblical counseling and spirit-filled prayers helped me respond and not react to the vicissitudes of life. Thank you, Reverend, for allowing the Holy Spirit to use you to help me complete this book. And thank you for writing one of the Forwards. I appreciate you greatly.

My thanks to all precious coaching clients, especially Dr BJ Jarmon, Dr Adriene Wright, Yasmeen Neil and Jade Miller, for allowing me to speak into your lives and for evoking the excellence you possess within for transforming not only your lives but also the lives of others in the Kingdom. My experience with you over this past year has been golden. God used you not only to help me crystalize the focus and the content of this book but also during this second year of the Covid-19 pandemic; you encouraged me to keep focused not on the external environmental challenges we all faced but to continue to let the Holy Spirit bring out the very best in me despite the challenges. I was able to respond rather than react. The result is this amazing work which I dedicate to each one of you.

My special thanks to my committed prayer partners Alice Imoh, and Rhonda Melton for praying me through to complete this work. The book is dedicated to you, especially the chapter on prayer, which deals with the important role prayer plays in transforming our lives into the best version of ourselves, particularly prayer directed by the Spirit of God.

Last but not the least, with this book, I thank God for bringing Dr Sherrie Walton, my book Writing Coach, into my life at this time. It would take another chapter in this book to share with the reading audience how precious you have been to me. Thank you for being the powerful woman of God you are for putting God first in all of our coaching conversations. I said yes to you being my book coach in our first encounter when I discovered that you have an intimate relationship with God and understood the important role the Holy Spirit plays in the life of every believer. I would not have been able to do that great focused outline without your understanding of who He is. Thanks for all your prophetic prayers throughout this one year journey. I could not have accomplished this work without your coaching and your prayers. Our work has just begun. Yes, we will write many more books together for the glory of and the expansion of the Kingdom of God.

Rev. Dr. Maureen McIntosh-Alberts, Ph.D.

Rev. Dr. Maureen McIntosh- Alberts is a Behavioral Scientist, Human and Organizational Development Systems Specialist that specializes in the Management of Change in Multicultural Organizations.

Dr. Alberts has lived, worked and traveled extensively in the Caribbean, Latin America, Europe and Africa while working with The World Bank, Washington, DC for 25 years, leading organizational change management interventions, coaching, mentoring and training staff in diversity equity and inclusion.

In addition she is a Certified Leadership Coach, Diversity Equity and Inclusion Trainer, Executive Director, John Maxwell Certified Coach, Speaker and Trainer, DISC Certified Personality Assessment Trainer and an Ambassador For The John Maxwell Group.

Dr. Maureen is the Founder and CEO of Zorbas Orphans Fund, a 501(c)(3), a charitable organization dedicated to empowering the minds of orphans and vulnerable youths for the future and to free girls from sex trafficking.

She's also the founder and CEO of The International Center for Empowerment and Leadership where she coaches, mentors, trains and facilitates personal, professional, emotional, financial and spiritual growth and development in the lives of faith-based leaders.

Dr. Maureen is passionate about empowering women of color in leadership to become the best version of themselves. She currently supervises leadership development coaching and mentoring labs where she helps them develop the resilient mindset required to fulfill their life calling and purpose courageously.

She conducts a financial literacy program designed to teach Biblical Principles for financial prosperity to faith-based leaders and members of the Body of Christ globally.

Rev. Dr. Maureen Alberts is also an ordained Minister, currently serving at One God Ministry in Fairfax, VA.

She has a son, Paul, who is married to Michelle. She is a grandmother to 16-year-old grandson, Aidan and currently lives in Alexandria, Virginia.

www.ingramcontent.com/pod-product-compliance
Lightning Source LLC
Chambersburg PA
CBHW071329120626
46546CB00002B/497